THE NOISE OF
DRUMS AND TRUMPETS

The First Great War Correspondent: William Howard Russell
during the Crimean War (photographed by Roger Fenton)

THE NOISE OF
DRUMS AND TRUMPETS

W.H.Russell reports from the Crimea

◉ ◉ ◉

ELIZABETH GREY

Henry Z. Walck, Inc.   New York

Copyright © Elizabeth Grey 1971

All rights reserved

ISBN 0-8098-3101-5

Library of Congress Catalog Card Number: 72-188901

947.7   Grey, Elizabeth
  G   The noise of drums and trumpets; W. H.
         Russell reports from the Crimea.
         Walck, 1972
           255p. illus. maps.

           First pub. in Great Britain in 1971.
         A graphic account of the Crimean War
         as shown in the dispatches sent from the
         scene by a war correspondent.

         1. Crimean War, 1853-1856   2. Russell,
         William Howard   I. Title

This Main Entry catalog card may be reproduced without permission

Printed in Great Britain by Butler & Tanner Ltd
Frome and London

This book
is
gratefully dedicated
to
JEAN MAULDON
who always has the answers . . .

Contents

Contents

NOTE

⊚ in the text indicates the beginning and end of direct quotations from Russell's dispatches and other sources. Russell's spelling has been retained except in a few instances where it was necessary to make minor changes to avoid confusion over place-names, or to clarify a word.

List of Illustrations

Acknowledgements

The author would like to express her sincere gratitude to Mr W. R. A. Easthope, past Archivist, and to Mr J. Gordon Phillips, present Archivist, of *The Times*, for their unfailing interest and help in the preparation of this book.

The publishers gratefully acknowledge permission to reproduce the following illustrations in this book:
Those which appear on pages 20, 32, 35, 43, 50, 52, 97, 99, 103, 115, 121, 125, 165, 167, 169, 209, 214, 219, 222, 230 and the Frontispiece are from The Radio Times Hulton Picture Library; the paintings on pages 47, 64, 129, 133, 155, 198, 212 are by Sir Henry Clifford V.C. and are now in the private collection of Nicholas Fitzherbert; the photograph on page 162 is courtesy of the Gernsheim Collection.

Maps

The Maps are by John Flower

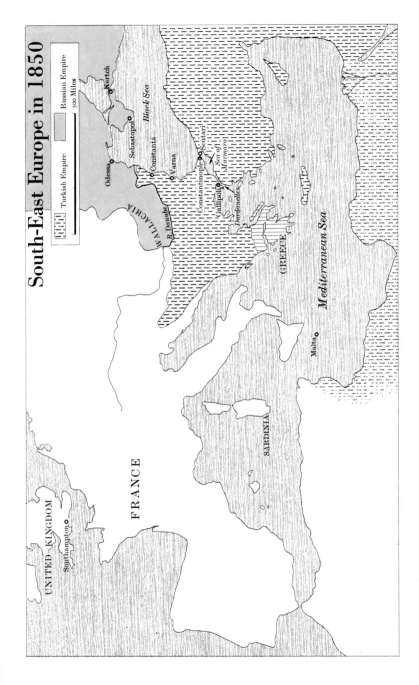

South-East Europe in 1850

Turkish Empire
Russian Empire
500 Miles

UNITED KINGDOM
Southampton

FRANCE

SARDINIA

Mediterranean Sea

Malta

GREECE

Gallipoli
Dardanelles
Scutari
Constantinople
Sea of Marmara

R. Danube

Varna
Constanta

WALLACHIA

Odessa

Sebastopol

Black Sea

Kertch

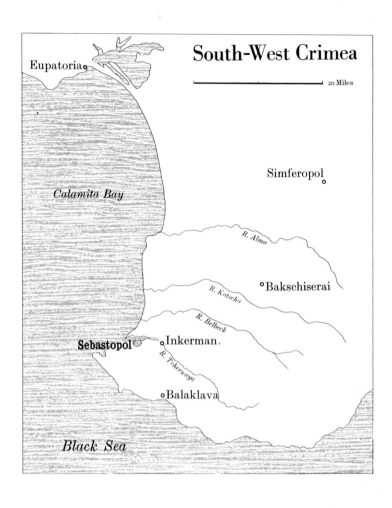

South-West Crimea

20 Miles

Eupatoria

Calamita Bay

Simferopol

R. Alma

R. Katscha

Bakschiserai

R. Belbeck

Sebastopol

Inkerman.

R. Tchernaya

Balaklava

Black Sea

. . . and he smelled the battle afar off, the thunder of the
captains, and the shouting.

Old Testament: Job, XXXIX, 25

. . . I wonder what would have come of it all had I
followed the quiet path . . . instead of those noisy drums
and trumpets . . .

William Howard Russell (1882)

Introduction:

A new kind of journalist

This is a story of a man who went to war, but never wore a uniform; won battles but never fired a shot; helped bring down a Government Minister—though he never sat in Parliament; shattered the smug complacency of a whole self-satisfied generation. His only weapons were a pen and a pad of paper. His name was William Howard Russell. He wrote for *The Times* of London.

Ever since man first communicated with man battles and wars have been described in every possible way: by poets, dramatists, and song-writers; by dry-as-dust historians (names and dates and statistics); by generals in dispatches and simple soldiers in their letters home. Every one of them has in some way distorted the truth. The poets and song-writers have glamorised, the historians hidden the human misery behind a barrage of facts, the generals inflated their successes and minimised their routs; the soldiers, seeing little beyond their boot-toes, have flattened great events with platitudes. Russell, detached yet wholly involved, brought a fresh, critical, intelligent eye, an articulate voice and a warm heart to an old, old story.

His life spanned almost a century; and what a century of upheaval and progress it was. He was born in the spring of 1820, a bare two months after the Prince Regent succeeded his father, 'mad' King George III. He died a few years before World War One. During his long life almost everything changed in a way and with a speed things had never changed before. The Industrial Revolution brought an explosion of technology. Engineers, builders and inventors seemed to strike a new, rich vein of imagination and drive. They made better roads, canals, railways. Steam power was harnessed to all sorts of industrial processes. Gas gave way to electricity; electricity led the way to the telegraph and telephone. Printing machines improved vastly.

In Britain there was also a great new burst of energy in the field of literature. Dickens, Thackeray, Trollope, the Brontë sisters, George Eliot and many others were producing enormous quantities of work. At the same time another sort of writing—journalism—was developing both technically and professionally. With improved machines newspapers were being printed more quickly and in greater numbers. The spread of education increased the demand for more up-to-date and accurate news, and its collection and narration came more and more to be recognised as a craft in its own right.

Russell was one of the 'new' journalists: very much a man of his time, sharing its tremendous energy and industry. He started his reporting life in the horse-and-carriage era, and ended it not long before the invention of the tank.

News had been sent back to English newspapers from far-away countries since the sixteenth century, but always as a side-line to some other job, by diplomats, travelling merchants, wealthy adventurers or explorers—and in the form of government handouts. It was not until the early years of the nineteenth century that *The Times* (which had done more than any other newspaper to speed the advance in newspaper technology) decided to send out an employee of its own, specifically to collect and report news from other countries.

Henry Crabb Robinson, a lawyer, was their first choice; he went to Germany in 1807. A year later, twelve years before Russell was born, he became the first official war correspondent when he was sent to Spain during the Napoleonic Wars, to cover the Battle of Corunna.

He was not an energetic reporter; he based his dispatches on translations from local papers rather than personal observation. On the evening of Britain's defeat of the French he did not even report the death of the British Commander-in-Chief, Sir John Moore. Not long afterwards he returned to England and his profession as a lawyer.

The all-powerful Duke of Wellington, however, did not relish even this mild and inaccurate reporting; no correspondents were allowed on later Peninsular campaigns, and there was no Russell—or even Robinson—to describe the Battle of Waterloo.

But *The Times* was undeterred. Despite Robinson's shortcomings it was obvious that a professional journalist on the spot, specially employed by the paper, was more likely to give readers a true and vivid account than any number of government reports and irregular, amateur dispatches. By the time Russell, as a young law student picking up a little money 'on the side', began reporting political events from his native Ireland in the 1840s, the principle of foreign, and war, reporting was established. He was not the only correspondent to describe the scandalous events of the Crimean War (even *The Times* had others) but, significantly, it is his name which is remembered.

What made him so outstanding, so different, so memorable —and so influential—was the combination of his personality, his brilliance as a journalist, and the extraordinary nature of the first great war he reported. It was a rare, almost miraculous, example of the coming together of the occasion, the opportunity, and the man who could use both to change a nation's attitudes. When it was over, many things were never to be the same again.

He was lucky in his newspaper. *The Times* was at that period at the height of its power, frequently in a position to

Times Cartoon—'On Brave Horse!' 'Our Own Correspondent
on his gallant charger "Dareall".'

control events; and its Editor, John Delane, stood staunchly
behind his Special Correspondent. The paper's leading
articles were every bit as forceful as Russell's dispatches. In
fact many people came to believe, quite wrongly, that
Russell wrote them himself!

The Times, though, was equally lucky in its new Correspondent. Russell was a frustrated soldier—a man who in
a curious way loved war, but hated what it did to the men
who fought it; and hated almost more the petty incompetence which set the helpless lower ranks unnecessarily at
risk and caused them needless suffering.

Unlike his predecessors and many contemporaries he was
never prepared to take things at their face value—to believe
all he was told. He seemed to smell out weakness, indifference, deception, stupidity, and he fearlessly exposed them.
His early reports, which read like 'instant history', came as a
considerable shock to the self-confident, Empire-backed,
Victorian middle-class into whose lace curtained drawing-
rooms he brought the blood and filth and agony, destroying
for ever the picture of war as a sort of gentlemanly contest,

acted out in some remote place where men died tidily with romantic last messages on their lips.

He was a big, jolly, impulsive Irishman with a great many of the traditional Irish strengths and weaknesses: outspoken to a fault, and sometimes hasty in his judgements, especially when his indignation was aroused. He was feckless with money and occasionally muddle-headed. But he exuded charm and affability. His capacity to make personal friends was invaluable in a job which few around him understood; which aroused the greatest suspicion and resentment in those in authority and often exposed him to violent attacks. He was more than once accused of giving information to an enemy by writing in too much detail about the conduct and progress of a war; and he aroused the American press to a fury by his criticism of both sides in their Civil War.

In the Crimea (and later, in America) he was given virtually no help and was often deliberately obstructed in his efforts to tell the truth as he saw it. But he was unstoppable.

He shared everything with the troops—the muck and dust, rain, snow, gales, blistering sun; the danger, boredom, and sheer discomfort of war; cramped voyages in overcrowded, smelly ships; bone-wearying treks across difficult country; hair-raising clashes with the enemy in which he was totally unprotected. He was wounded, not once, but several times.

He might not have been the absolute first, but he was the first of a new kind of war journalist: the kind which laid the foundations for today's war reporting, but which itself more or less died with the development and spread of the telegraph and telephone. For once these contraptions became widely established there was no more time for writing the long, detailed and evocative reports which Russell produced; and once it was realised how potentially damaging his revelations of troop movements and the like could be, censorship was (often rightly) imposed.

Of his own type of correspondent he wrote: 'I sat by his birth and I followed him to his grave.'

Fed as we are today on shock headlines and staccato reports, his literary style strikes us perhaps as extravagant and flowery, even quaint, but he was writing in a comparatively leisurely age, when there was little to compete with the written word for attention. There was no television or radio, newspapers carried no photographs and few other illustrations; and so the painting of a picture in words was still part of the journalist's craft.

But, however verbose, Russell was—and still is—rivetingly readable; a master of vivid description. He had a quite extraordinary eye for detail, and the ability to describe it. Although he wrote brilliantly about battles, it was the soldiers' day-to-day life which he brought home to his readers—not only the mud and blood, but the uniforms they wore, the country they passed through, the weather they endured, the food they ate.

Through this gift he made those who stayed at home share in events, dramatic and mundane, which happened hundreds —sometimes thousands—of miles away. And because he made them share in the small things, when he had something important or shocking to say, they listened.

This book is about Russell's first—his Crimean War— adventure; but it is not unduly preoccupied with tactics, strategy and battle. Like Russell himself it is concerned with the victims and their everyday lives, the mistakes and tragedy of war (and the fantastic, sometimes heartbreakingly useless, acts of personal heroism which have made war one of the great newspaper 'stories' of all time) and also the good which sometimes comes out of evil.

It is largely one man's view of what happened. A great deal of it is told in Russell's own stirring words.

1

The sound of drums and trumpets

It all began, literally, to the sound of drums and trumpets, in the early spring of 1854. One by one the regiments of Guards, in the full splendour of their ridiculous uniforms, swung through London—bands playing, rows of little drummer-boys thrumming out their blood-stirring call.

Reporters from the London press were there. For readers not able to join the crowds packing the streets, *Bell's Weekly Messenger* described the thrilling scene as the Scots Guards left their barrack *en route* for Southampton:

⊙ Precisely at seven o'clock the barrack gates were thrown open, and the Guards commenced their march in slow time . . . down Birdcage Walk, and into the esplanade in front of the Palace.

At the head of the column marched the splendid regimental band, playing 'Oh Where, and Oh Where is my Highland laddie gone?'. The plaintive and rather melancholy air of which gave, for the moment, an impression of solemnity to the whole scene which well became the occasion.

But this feeling was only momentary, as the instant the troops began to pass in front of the Palace, the crowd outside the railings commenced such deafening cheers as quite drowned the notes of the whole band.

Amid such marks of enthusiasm the regiment steadily pursued its way . . . In front of the Palace the whole force presented arms as one man—the colours were lowered—the officers saluted—the band tried to play 'God Save the Queen', but were fairly hushed by the cheers of the crowd . . .

Outside Buckingham Palace: the departure of the Guards for
the Crimea at the start of the war

After this . . . the regiment again marched forward tolerably quiet though as each company passed the Royal party,
the same scene of vociferous cheering was renewed on a
small scale.

At length the regiment emerged upon the Mall . . . at the
National Gallery, round St Martin's Church and in Trafalgar
Square, crowds had gathered which greeted the troops as
they swept into the Strand with a cheer which was tremendous . . . ⊙

The cheering continued all the way down to the coast, but
with the final departure of the troopships came the first
ominous cracks in the glossy façade of the British Army
organisation.

Preparations for sailing took place in the early hours of the
morning when all the decent, optimistic citizens who had
cheered the marching soldiers on their way were in bed, and
unable to see the chaos which reigned on the quayside. The

bands were silent now, but there was noise enough—from Petty Officers shouting (and countermanding) orders, from seamen and dockers feverishly trying to rush last minute stores aboard, and from the raucous singing of the troops, celebrating victory even before war had been declared.

In the darkness lanterns flared, only to plunge the shadowed corners where boxes of vital equipment stood unnoticed into deeper gloom. Men stumbled, swearing, over bollards, ropes, inebriated soldiers, weeping wives and sweethearts, shapeless bundles, handcarts, and each other. Finally, with how-much-nobody-knew left behind, the ships sailed.

It was not the first, or last, chaotic departure. Only a week before, on February 23rd, amid similar scenes, three troopships filled with Guards had sailed out of Southampton bound for Malta and the eastern Mediterranean. Others left from ports as widely separated as Leith, Portsmouth and Woolwich.

William Howard Russell, Special Correspondent of *The Times*, went too—still sharing the British nation's illusion that he was about to report the triumph of 'the finest, most powerful army in the modern world'.

Russell was thirty-three at the time—a buccaneer-in-Establishment-clothing: large, genial, bearded, with dark hair curling around his ears, a mouth quick to curve into a smile, and eyes often alight with mischief but capable when he was suspicious or angry of narrowing to piercing slits.

His journalistic experience was already wide, ranging from the reporting of the Irish parliamentary elections and the trial of the Irish rebel O'Connor (undertaken to subsidise his Law studies), to descriptions of the Great Exhibition of 1851 and the Duke of Wellington's funeral.

He had served a stint as a parliamentary reporter at Westminster, and already seen something of warfare as an observer of the 1850 Schleswig-Holstein rebellion, a brief but angry quarrel between the Danes and Germans. He had even been wounded, slightly but, as it turned out, significantly, for his experience aroused a sympathetic interest in the treatment of the battle-wounded which was to remain as strong as his interest in battle itself.

And so, although he had not originally intended to be a journalist, he was already practised in his craft when he left on what was to become—for himself, his newspaper, and the people of Britain—a shattering experience.

He set off with his Editor's cheerful promise of 'an easy and pleasant trip' (and a certain return by Easter!), leaving behind his Irish wife Mary and a clutch of small children. Four days before sailing, a boisterous send-off party was given for him by his London friends, who included Charles Dickens and William Thackeray. Much wine was drunk, and some rather dreadful verse composed and sung in his honour.

The Government of the day was less enthusiastic about his departure on what was then a novel mission. His 'permission to sail' mysteriously never arrived at Southampton, and a letter of introduction from Lord Hardinge, Commander-in-Chief of the Army, was astonishingly met with suspicion.

Undeterred by authority's hostile indifference he began, immediately the troopships left England, to write the first of his vivid descriptions, not only of the great moments of the war, but the homely, sometimes humorous, details of everyday life which made the high moments and the tragedies more poignant by contrast:

⊙ Soon after daylight anchors were tripped, and with full steam off dashed the little fleet ... They ran past the Needles at 8.15, and were soon bowling along with a fresh breeze on the bow in weather which sailors by some strange perversity of the usual terms relating to the state of the atmosphere denominated 'moderate to fine'.

The breeze was, with all deference to naval authority,

strong and boisterous, but with the excitement and novelty of the situation, the mind ruled the stomach, and the men evinced the usual degree of anxiety as to the time for eating and drinking, which shows that the nastiest and most anti-gastric of all maladies had not seized them.

The crews of the ships busied themselves swinging hammocks for the men. Fourteen inches is man-of-war allowance, but eighteen inches was allowed for the Guards. The hammocks were not strictly luxurious: they consisted of the usual canvas, one blanket, and the military overcoat for those that liked to use it.

Knapsack-stowing was wondrous work for a time, but even it palled after an hour or so, and there was nothing but looking at seagulls, smoking pipes, watching each other smoke, and 'wondering if they were going to be sick' . . .

On Friday, the long swell from the westward began to tell upon the troops. The figureheads plunged deeply into the waters and the heads of the poor soldiers hung despondingly over gunwale, portsill, stay and mess-tin, as their bodies bobbed to and fro with the swaying, creaking, tumbling tabernacle in which they were encamped.

It was satisfactory to see that the paroxysms of the complaint were more characterised by resolute torpor and a sullen determination 'to do or die' than by the ecstatic misery of the Frenchman, or the prostrate inanity of the German.

At night they brightened up, and when the bugles sounded at nine o'clock nearly all were able to crawl into their hammocks for sleep . . . ◉

The next day the high seas died down and the men felt ◉ a sense of joyfulness for release from the clutches of their enemy so strong that they cheered a grampus which blew close alongside, in reply to a stentorian demand for 'three cheers for the jolly old whale!' ◉

The atmosphere became almost one of holiday—at least

for the men. Below decks the scene was more sombre. Battened down and crammed together in a long, dim, vault-like hold, hideously hot and stinking of ammonia and vinegar, the pride of the Cavalry regiments faced each other in two ranks across a double row of wooden mangers, each horse secured round belly and shoulders by canvas slings to steady it against the roll of the ship. But only against the gentlest movement, and certainly not against panic and sickness. During the long hours of the storm the terrified animals reared and plunged, jerking at the restraining slings until their hides were galled and bleeding.

The hold when the storm had blown itself out was a shambles. At least five horses died. Luckily the rest of the ten-day voyage to Malta was smooth, and, like the men, the remaining horses gradually recovered.

At Malta the ships disgorged their restless cargo, and almost at once Russell began to see—and report—the flaws in organisation which were to bedevil the army throughout the campaign.

⊙ It were well indeed [he wrote severely] if things on shore were as well managed as they have been at sea; but, strange as it may appear, some of the men left their floating prisons only to relinquish comforts to which they had a right, and have had to 'rough it' on *terra firma* with greater patience and endurance than they were called upon to exercise while on board the steamers.

To speak the truth, 'somebody' is to blame for placing any of Her Majesty's forces in such a position that they had had to endure some of the minor inconveniences of warfare before their time.

Complaints are made that such a regiment was left without coals—that another had no lights or candles—that another has suffered from exposure to cold at night under canvas, when they ought to have been under cover of a more substantial nature—that in some cases that terrible calamity, short commons, actually fell upon a portion of the men and that forage was not to be had for the officers' horses.

The commissariat are blamed for these deficiencies, but they are said to declare that they received no proper instructions ... The despatch of these troops was determined several months ago; the precise mode and the very time of their arrival could be calculated to a day or two; and therefore, if the complaints to which I have alluded are well founded, serious blame rests in some quarter or other, and there is no use in trying to evade it by shifting it from shoulder to shoulder ... ⊙

It was the first salvo from Russell's own artillery.

Meanwhile more and more official troops were arriving, some of them French. The uniform worn by the Zouave (who came from North Africa but who was in fact French) was, if anything, even more elaborate and unsuitable for battle than that worn by the nineteenth-century British fighting man. According to the indefatigable Mr Russell he wore:

⊙ ... a sort of red fez cap with a turban of white or green rolled round it to protect the head; a jacket of blue cloth with red facings, decorated with some simple ornaments and open in front, so as to display the throat.

Round his waist a broad sash was folded several times, so as to keep up the ample pantaloons and to support the back. The pantaloons, of scarlet cloth, fit closely over the hips, and then expand to the most Dutchman-like dimensions, till they are gathered just below the knee in loose bagging folds, so that they look almost like a kilt.

From the knee to the ankle the leg is protected by greaves made of stout, yellow-embroidered leather (with black stripes), laced down the back and descending to the ankle, where it is met by a white gaiter which nearly covers the shoe.

The whole costume is graceful, easy and picturesque ... ⊙

But hardly suited to its purpose! If anything demonstrates the complete lack of understanding of what lay ahead, it is surely the garb in which the men went to meet it.

But then, nobody really expected to fight. Even Mr Russell did not believe it. In a letter to his wife he wrote from the Maltese port of Valletta;

⊙ I am glad to tell you it is generally believed that our troops will never see a shot fired, and that the war, or whatever it is, will be over by the summer . . . ⊙

Soldiers continued to pour into Malta, and the tension increased to snapping point. When finally, on March 28th (Russell's thirty-fourth birthday), war on Russia was officially declared and the troops began to re-embark:

⊙ . . . the excitement produced in the island was almost indescribable. Crowds of people assembled on the shores of the harbours and lined the quays and public landing places, the crash of military music being almost drowned in the enthusiastic cheers of the soldiers; the leave-taking by the officers and men of their wives and families formed a painful contrast to the joy which otherwise so generally prevailed.

As the vessels moved slowly from their buoys dense masses of people lined the batteries, and yet denser crowds of soldiers the forts, cheering their comrades as the vessels glided along, the cheers from one fort being taken up by the troops in the others, and as joyously responded to from those on board. ⊙

The refusal of the authorities to acknowledge Russell's right to travel as a newspaper reporter with the troops from England had been the first hint that all was not to run smoothly for him. His second setback occurred just before he left Malta.

This time he had been (reluctantly) offered a passage on the *Golden Fleece*, which carried the Rifle Brigade. He had engaged a Maltese servant to go with him, and left the man to bring the baggage on board. Just before sailing the man begged, with tears in his eyes, for a small advance of his wages 'to leave with his wife and tree little children . . .' Russell never saw him, or his baggage, again, and finally sailed with little more than the clothes he was wearing—and of course his notebook.

But it took more than the loss of all his possessions to divert this sharp-eyed observer's attention from what was going on around him. The rôle of that strange animal the War Correspondent was less firmly defined than it is today— it was in fact what the individual made it, and everything was grist to Russell's mill. He merely reported what he saw, and added his own uninhibited comments. During the voyage his mind was far from the carnage to come. He noted with almost child-like delight that:

⊙ . . . many small birds fluttered on the yards, masts and bulwarks, plumed their little jaded wings, and after a short rest, impelled by an inscrutable instinct, launched themselves once more across the bosom of the deep.

Some of them were common titlarks, others little greyish buntings, others yellow and black fellows. They were agreeable visitors, and served to afford much entertainment to Jack and the soldiers.

Three of the owls and a titlark were introduced to each other in a cage, and the ship's cat was thrown in by way of making an impromptu 'happy family'. Pussy obstinately refused to hold any communication with the owls—they seemed in turn to hate each other, and all evinced determined animosity toward the unfortunate titlark, which speedily languished and died . . . ⊙

During another storm several ships ran for shelter off the south coast of Greece, and anchors were dropped in Vatika Bay . . .

⊙ This little flotilla evidently alarmed the inhabitants very much, for the few who were fishing in boats fled to shore.

27

No doubt the apparition in the bay of such a force, flying the tricolour and the union jack, and so hastily assembled, frightened the people. They could be seen running to and fro along the shore like ants when their nest is stirred. ⊙

These very understandable fears apparently died down when the armada took no aggressive action, for:

⊙ At dusk our bands played the popular dance music of the day, and the mountains of the Mores, for the first time since they rose from the sea to watch the birth of Venus, echoed the strains of 'God Save the Queen'.

The people lighted bonfires, as if by way of signal, upon the hills, but the light soon died out. Our vocalists re-assembled, and sang glees or fine vigorous choruses together and the night passed pleasantly in smooth water and on an even keel . . . ⊙

The expedition's immediate destination was Gallipoli—a peninsula which forms the European shore of the Dardanelles, a narrow strip of water joining the Mediterranean to the Sea of Marmara, which in its turn is joined to the Black Sea by the narrow Bosphorus.

Landfall was made late on the night of April 4th. Early the next morning the first problems began to present themselves.

⊙ . . . a boat came off from the shore with two commissariat officers and an interpreter. They informed us that the Consul had gone up the Dardanelles to look for us, but that he would return in the course of the day, and added the unwelcome news that horses were not to be had at any price, that provisions were not very cheap, and that the French, having arrived first, had got hold of the best part of the town, and of the best quarters as well . . . ⊙

In fact all that was left for the British troops was a small town eight miles away, according to Russell '. . . a wretched place—picturesque to a degree, but horribly uncomfortable . . . '

2
Spoiling for a fight

What was it that had sent so many troops off to this distant, exotic, and 'horribly uncomfortable' part of the world in a blare of noise, clamour of gaudy colour, gold braid, flashing swords; and on such a wave of jubilation?

The root cause of war is never simple, but like so many others this one was sparked off by a quite small, comparatively unimportant, incident in one of the most unlikely places imaginable: Bethlehem. It was, at least in the early stages, a religious war; or more accurately a religious squabble—a sort of holy 'who does what' dispute.

At this time in its chequered career the Holy Land was part of a crumbling Turkish Empire, though many other countries, through their religious interests, claimed 'rights' there; in particular the Roman Catholics—supported by France—and the Orthodox Church—backed by Russia.

In the summer of 1853 some Roman Catholic monks decided to fix a silver star over the manger in the Church of the Nativity. The Orthodox monks tried to stop them. A fight broke out, and several Orthodox monks were killed. The Russians were furious with the Turkish police for not keeping order, and even hinted that the Turks had connived at the 'murders'.

In fact Russia had for some time been seeking an excuse to disrupt the Turkish Empire (which at that time included Yugoslavia, Bulgaria and Greece, and most of the Asian part of the Middle East), take over some of its territories, and so break through from the Black Sea into the Mediterranean;

perhaps even further, overland to India and the great trade routes.

The thought of the Great Bear reaching out its huge paws in their direction frightened both France and Britain, and when a squadron of the Czar's navy based on the port of Sebastopol in the Crimea attacked a Turkish flotilla and sank every ship (shooting many of the sailors as they struggled in the water), first France, and then Britain (only twenty-four hours later) declared war on Russia. The pretence was that they were protecting a weak nation. In fact they were protecting themselves.

The truth was that, fear of Russia apart, both countries were spoiling for a fight. France still smarted from the defeats of the Napoleonic army forty years earlier whilst Britain, with the great victory of Waterloo still rosy in her memory, was anxious to add further laurels to her battle-crown. In addition, the people of Britain—especially the increasingly prosperous and influential middle-class—felt that to support an army which had not fought a war for more than a generation was an extravagance. The soldiers were there, 'eating their heads off' so to speak, and should be made to fight—or at least do *something*—for their living . . . and the greater glory of Victorian Britain.

The two nations were unlikely allies, but fear is a great unifier and both felt they had much to lose by a Russian occupation of the eastern Mediterranean; and since the war was to be fought a long way off, by professional soldiers, only very few people were personally touched by it—at least to begin with.

And so the Great Adventure, which was for Britain to become the Great Disaster, began—as badly as it was to continue.

The mismanagement which had first shown itself on the Southampton docks, and then in Malta, reached a new peak in Gallipoli. The contrast with the good organisation of the

French was marked. Not only were the French—the first comers—best served but, by the time the British arrived after midnight, there was not even a pilot to show the ships where to anchor, and:

⊙ ... there was something depressing in this silent reception of the first British army that ever landed on the shores of these straits. When morning came the tricolour was floating right and left and the blue coats of the French were well marked on the shore, the long lines of bullock carts stealing along the strand towards their camp making it evident that they were taking care of themselves. ⊙

Three days later Russell wrote an indignant letter to his Editor in London:

⊙ The management is infamous, and the contrast offered by our proceedings to the conduct of the French most painful. Could you believe it—the sick have not a bed to lie upon? They are landed and thrown into a ricketty house without a chair or table in it. The French with their ambulances, excellent commissariat staff ... etc. in every respect are immeasurably our superiors.

While these things go on, Sir George Brown* only seems anxious about the men being clean-shaved, their necks well stiffened, the waist belts tight. He insists on officers and men being in full fig; no loose coats, jackets etc. His wonderful pack kills the men, as the weight is so disposed as to hang from, instead of resting on the shoulders ... ⊙

Perhaps just a little of Russell's bitterness arose from his own brusque treatment at the hands of Sir George, who 'took no notice of me the whole time I was on board ... ' and 'offered me no facilities'.

He goes on, irritably:

⊙ I run a good chance of starving if the army takes the field. ... I have no tent, nor can I get one without an order, and even if I had one I doubt very much whether Sir George

* Commander of the Light Division

31

Sir George Brown and his staff (Roger Fenton)

Brown would allow me to pitch it within the camp. All my efforts to get a horse have been unsuccessful. I cannot get out of the camp, for 17 miles a day with a letter to write would soon knock up Hercules.

I am living in a pig-sty, without chair, table, stool, or window glass, and an old hag of sixty to attend to me who doesn't understand a word I say. I live on eggs and brown bread, sour Tenedos wine, and onions and rice.

The French have the place to themselves ... ◉

What was *wrong* with the British army? Why was it so inefficient?

To begin with, it was forty years since the victory of Waterloo, and for those forty years Britain had lived on the memory, and the belief, that any army which could defeat Napoleon was invincible. As Waterloo receded it became even more glorious in the memory.

At the same time cuts were made in all the services essential to the efficient running of an army even in peace-time. Not only were there too few soldiers to fight a war properly but the departments which supplied them had been run down, and there was too little transport of every kind to carry the enormous amount of equipment, food, clothes and medical supplies necessary.

The artillery was deficient, out of date, and in some cases needed repairing. There was so much overlapping of responsibility, both in the army itself and the government departments which controlled it, that very often its right hand hardly knew what its left hand was doing.

Worst of all, perhaps, those who were to direct it in the field were hopelessly inexperienced. Very few had done any actual fighting. For forty years the army had been a prestige profession run largely by amateur officers. Rich young men bought themselves commissions—and promotion—in fashionable regiments, and strutted about in their stage-musical uniforms like peacocks. The official price of a lieutenant-colonelcy in a Cavalry regiment was £7,250, but so eagerly was the command of a regiment sought by the young 'bloods' that they would pay five or six times as much.

They were often brave fighters—there are examples of great personal (though often useless and unnecessary) courage shown by officers in the Crimea—but they treated war as a personal contest, a sort of game, and the men who served under them were merely pawns ... almost personal possessions, to be moved about, dressed (often at the officer's expense) in showy uniforms one better than the next regiment; mounted, if the regiment were cavalry, on splendid horses; but never for a moment considered as human beings.

Their living-quarters even at home were, by present-day standards, appalling—airless and foul-smelling, with no facilities for drying clothes when the men came off duty in bad weather. Their diet, too, was monotonous and inadequate (largely boiled meat and stale bread). Tuberculosis was a more frequent cause of death than combat in the years between Waterloo and the Crimea.

If they disobeyed the often absurd and over-rigid rules they were flogged until the blood ran from their backs.

The result was that the ranks were filled with drop-outs, throw-outs, sub-criminals, the unemployable, the desperate and the recklessly adventurous. When war was declared on Russia the gaps were hastily filled with extra 'volunteers', not all of whom were as enthusiastic for the expedition as they might have been.

Leading this ramshackle army was the only man who had had any real experience of a fighting war: Lord Raglan was a brave soldier and a conscientious leader, but had spent his professional life from the age of nineteen in the shadow of that military giant the Duke of Wellington, as the great man's Military Secretary. For forty years they were as close as father and son. They even looked alike.

On the field of Waterloo Lieutenant Colonel Lord Fitzroy Somerset (as Lord Raglan then was) received a smashing blow from a musket ball on his right elbow. Without fuss he walked to the field hospital and climbed on to a table for the surgeon to operate. His arm was removed above the elbow, without anaesthetic, and he did not even groan, but as the orderly tossed aside his severed arm he called out: 'Hey, bring my arm back. There's a ring my wife gave me on the finger . . .'

Brave and conscientious he was, but having acted always as second fiddle to a military genius, the job Lord Raglan was given in 1854 was too big for him. At sixty-five he was

Lord Raglan (Roger Fenton)

too old, and after forty years of peace his ideas were out of date. In the end it broke him. He died in the Crimea while the war was still undecided, some say of a broken heart.

At the outbreak of the war he was serving as Master-General of the Ordnance, the department responsible for equipment, fortifications and barracks—a job involving a great deal of desk and paper work. Such work was to dog him to his death. It was hardly good training for the command of thirty thousand fighting men, but there just was not, at that time, anyone else with his experience of warfare who was even as young as he was—and some of the lustre which surrounded the memory of the Iron Duke had rubbed off on his assistant.

The British people looked at him, and his army, through rose-tinted spectacles. Even Russell, in the very early days, painted an enthusiastic picture of a peace-time British soldier's life; a life in which he was:

⊙ . . . accustomed to the easy indolence of London taps, the unrestrained ease of Winchester bars, and the social military elegancies of Windsor, vying with the police itself in the intensity of their *entente cordiale* with the female servantry of London, living in large, airy, dry barracks, and provided with abundant well-cooked food . . . ⊙

But Russell learned fast, and the hard way—from personal experience. His own position was certainly invidious. In the field he was neither fish, flesh, fowl nor good red herring. Nobody wanted him, or knew what to do with him.

⊙ Lord Raglan [he reported bitterly] never spoke to me in his life . . . I was regarded as a mere camp follower, whom it would be impossible to take more notice of than you would of a crossing sweeper . . . ⊙

Everyone was suspicious of his motives. What was he doing there? Snooping? As soon as his dispatches began to appear in *The Times* it became obvious that he was, and he did not hesitate to be as outspoken in print as he had been in private letters to his chief.

It was not only those in authority on the spot who came in for his castigation.

⊙ The persons really culpable are those who sent them out without a proper staff and without the smallest foresight or consideration. Early and late these officers might be seen toiling amid a set of apathetic Turks and stupid araba drivers, trying in vain to make bargains and give orders in the language of signs, or aided by interpreters who understand neither the language of the contractor nor contractee. ⊙

It can have done him little good that he continued to stress the contrast with the well-organised French, who 'had a perfect baggage train and carried off all their stores and baggage to their camps the moment they landed . . . ' After all, this was the army Britain had defeated at Waterloo; it was humiliating that they should now be bossing the British army around, and getting in first every time.

After a somewhat blinkered start, Russell had foreseen the chaos to come in the most remarkable way which amounted almost to second-sight. From Malta, when the muddle and mismanagement first made itself clear, he had written:

◉ With our men well clothed, well fed, well housed (whether in camp or town does not much matter), and well attended to, there is little to fear ... But inaction might bring listlessness and despondency, and in their train disease ...

Let us have plenty of doctors. Let us have an overwhelming army of medical men to combat disease. Let us have a staff, full and strong, of young and active and experienced men. Do not suffer our soldiers to be killed by antiquated imbecility. Do not hand them over to the mercies of ignorant etiquette and effete seniority, but give the sick every chance which skill, energy and abundance of the best specifics can afford them ... ◉

If only somebody had listened. But some of his reports seem so incredible that perhaps, at the time, he was thought to be exaggerating—sensationalising. Of Sir George Brown and his insistence on the men's shaving, he wrote:

◉ His hatred of hair amounted to almost a mania. 'Where there is hair there is dirt, and where there is dirt there will be disease.' That is an axiom on which was founded a vigorous war against all capillary adornments and in vain engineers, exposed to all weathers, and staff officers, exhibit sore and bleeding lips; they must shave, no matter what the result is. The stocks (close-fitting leather neckbands worn inside the tunic collars) too were ordered to be kept up, stiff as ever.

On the march of the Rifles to their camp at least one man fell out of the ranks senseless; immediate recovery was effected by the simple process of opening the stock ... ◉

Astonishingly, Russell goes on to add of Sir George Brown that 'a kinder man to the soldiers, or one who looked more to their rights, never lived . . .'!

Hearing with distress that his correspondent was in difficulties—ignored, snubbed and obstructed; without suitable accommodation or decent food—Delane, the Editor of *The Times*, used his considerable authority in London and arranged with the Horse Guards that Russell should be allowed to accompany them, and to draw such rations as he needed.

He was not able to take advantage of this agreement until he reached Scutari, twin town to Constantinople on the Asian shore of the Bosphorus. Even then the 'agreement' did him little good, for on his return from one expedition he found his small tent had been pulled down and thrown out of the camp on the orders, according to his servant, of 'a brutal officer'.

This particular officer had been happy enough, in Malta, to give Russell the 'facilities' withheld by Sir George Brown, but by now Russell's first letter, describing the outrageous treatment of the sick on landing in Gallipoli, had been published, and searching questions asked in the House of Lords . . . Already he was making his presence felt in high places and nobody, except perhaps his Editor, was very pleased about it.

Unperturbed, he continued to send back voluminous reports to London, both for publication and in the form of personal letters to Delane who knew well how to make use of this private information.

The Times was at that period the mouthpiece for a large and vigorous new pressure group in Britain. The whole power-structure of the country was shifting. After centuries of almost unquestioned rule by the aristocracy a new commercial class, brought into being by the Industrial Revolution, was flexing its muscles and demanding more of a say in the running of the country. The aristocratic amateur officers, they felt, had already made a muddle of running the army. Now the ineptitude and inertia of the aristocratic politicians were beginning to show. The practical men of business were losing patience.

With Russell's dispatches as a weapon, *The Times* thundered out its condemnation of the Establishment direction of the war, agitating for control to be brought under the authority of a single Cabinet Minister.

The extent of the newspaper's power may be measured by the fact that on June 9th, 1854, Parliament announced the creation of a new Secretaryship of State for War.

The Times was not slow to point out to its readers that this was exactly what it had demanded.

3
Angry men and goaded cattle

April/May 1854. Nobody can have been sorry to leave Gallipoli, but the first arrival at Scutari* in mid-April was a bleak one; the hills behind Constantinople were covered with deep snow which, as Russell remarked, 'gave a curious shock to our notions of an Oriental spring'.

A bleakness of another kind descended on the men when at dawn they 'began to receive visits from Turks who were kind enough to see if they could relieve us of anything they thought we did not want'.

The huge barracks where they were installed were 'just as they had been left by the Turkish troops . . . inhabited in every nook and corner by legions of fleas and less active but

* Now known as Uskudar

more nauseous insects . . .'

These barracks were to become known the civilised world over when a part of them was turned into the hospital in which Florence Nightingale attempted the gargantuan task of nursing the sick and wounded flowing across the Black Sea from the Crimea.

In fact on that first occasion Russell stayed only a few days before returning to Gallipoli, where many of the troops still remained, to carry on his close observation of the everyday life of an army in waiting—and the inevitably damaging effect it has on the native life around it:

◉ Every day long strings of camels laden with skins of coarse red wine, raki and corn, might be seen stalking along the dusty roads and filing through the dingy bazaar, and wild-looking countrymen with droves of little shaggy ponies trooped in hour after hour to sell the produce they carried and the beasts that bore it.

They were corrupted already and had quite lost the simplicity of their mercantile notions. Instead of piastres, they began to demand lire, shillings, pounds and Napoleons, and they displayed ingenuity in the art of selling horses and doctoring them that would have done honour to a Yorkshireman.

Wine, which was formerly two or three piastres (4*d* or 5*d*) a bottle as an outside price, soon sold for 1*s* 6*d* or 2*s*. Meat was bad and dear, the beef being very like coarse mahogany; the mutton was rather better, but very lean. Milk was an article of the highest luxury and only to be seen on the tables of the great; and the sole attempt at butter was rancid lard packed in strong-smelling camel's hair bags.

It was really wonderful that no Englishman had sufficient enterprise to go out to Gallipoli with a stock of creature comforts and camp necessities. There was scarcely an article of common use in England which could not be disposed of at very considerable profit. ◉

It was more than a month after landing at Gallipoli, early in May, when news came of a Russian advance into northern Bulgaria. Then the Rifle Brigade, the 50th Regiment, the 93rd, 4th, 28th and 44th Regiments struck camp and made ready to move on to Scutari. The confusion was as great as ever. Nobody seemed to have learned anything.

◉ . . . the mass of baggage belonging to these regiments was enormous. The trains of buffalo and bullock carts, of pack-horses and mules, and of led-horses, which filed along the road seemed sufficient for the army of Xerxes.

For seven or eight miles the teams of country carts, piled up with beds and trunks and soldiers' wives and tents, were almost unbroken, and now and then an over-laden mule tumbled down, or a wheel came off, and the whole line of march became a confused struggle of angry men and goaded cattle . . . ◉

Although it was still early in the day, it was already very hot.

◉ . . . [the regiments] came on solid and compact as blocks of marble, the sun dancing on their polished bayonets and scarlet coats . . . All the men are as red in the face as turkeycocks—they seem to be gasping for breath . . . they are indeed sorely distressed for a rigid band of leather rendered quite relentless by fibres and buckles of brass is fixed tightly to their throats and their knapsacks are filled to the pitch of mortal endurance . . . the coat is buttoned tightly up also to aid the work of suffocation and the belts and buckles compress the unhappy soldier where he most requires ease and unrestricted play of the muscle . . . ◉

Once again the contrast with French organisation was glaring:

◉ . . . it became perceptible at a glance that pro rata they carried much less impedimenta than our regiments . . . it may be that the absence of women and the small kit of the French officers went far to account for it.

Frenchmen live in their uniform, while everybody knows no real British soldier is quite happy without his mufti. He must have his wideawake and shooting jacket, and a dressing-gown and evening-dress, and a tub of some sort . . . [and] a variety of gay shirting . . . ◉

A century later the imagination boggles at the idea of a soldier (even an officer) setting off to war complete with evening dress and 'a tub of some sort', particularly when so much other, and vital, equipment was missing; but the peculiar arrangements which put the officers into the positions they held at the time of Crimea resulted in their persisting in regarding war as a sort of glorified fox-hunting weekend.

Russell's reference to the 'absence of women' among the French troops is more surprising. At this period, although there were no women's services as we know them today, it was customary for a certain number of women to go with the army when it went to war.

The French were accompanied by *vivandières*—tough young women who, among other duties, sold provisions and wine to the troops. They were officially recognised, and disciplined. They even wore uniform (blue tunics and trousers and feathered hats). Perhaps because they were so tough, and officially recognised as part of the army, Russell hardly regarded them as women at all—though there is little doubt that the soldiers themselves were well aware of the fact!

As for the British army, it was customary for a certain number of soldiers' wives (an average of six to every hundred men) to go along as cooks, laundresses and amateur nurses. There was fierce competition for this 'privilege', and the coveted permits were decided by the drawing of lots.

The whole position of British soldiers' wives at this period was most unhappy. Only a small proportion of them were recognised at all. Ordinary soldiers needed to have permission from their Commanding Officers before they could marry. This given, the wives were, most reluctantly, 'taken on the strength'. If a soldier married without permission his wife and children, so far as the army was concerned, simply did not exist. There was no financial allowance, and no accommodation provided.

Even those on the strength had a rough time, sharing the barrack-room with their husbands—and the rest of the regiment—with no more privacy than a ragged curtain could afford.

They were 'allowed' to earn a little money by doing the regiment's laundry, but if the regiment went overseas and they were unlucky in the ballot, this stopped, and the plight of even recognised army wives became desperate. Hence the competition for permits to follow their men into battle, where they endured incredible hardship. A few who went to the Crimea earned fame and respect for their fortitude and courage under fire; others sank into complete degradation, or died in horrifying circumstances—sometimes giving birth to children among the mud and blood of the battlefield.

More surprisingly, a few 'ladies'—officers' wives—went to the Crimea too, notably Lady Erroll and Mrs Fanny Duberly, wife of the Paymaster of the 8th Hussars, who kept a diary

British Infantry in barracks at Gallipoli, late in 1854

throughout the Crimean campaign which is almost as vivid, if not so well-informed, as Russell's.

The rôle of these ladies was quite unproductive. They merely went for the excitement and fun—and to 'lend tone to the social functions'!

They were not alone in regarding war as merely a spectacle; there were also men on the battlefield who were nothing to do with the army—'Travelling Gentlemen', who cheered from the sidelines as though the whole thing were some sort of super football match.

Later in the campaign, during the bombardment of Sebastopol, regimental bands were detailed to play 'appropriate airs' to entertain these spectators during lulls in the fighting; and an enterprising shipping firm ran package tours from London. A fortnight's travel and accommodation, to include visits to Constantinople and the battlefields, cost five pounds.

May 1854. Scutari, south-east across the narrow neck of the Bosphorus from Constantinople,* was merely a base from which the allied forces were to operate. Once established there the Commanders-in-Chief decided that the Anglo-French contingent should 'contain' the Russians on the eastern bank of the River Danube, while the Turks advanced on their right flank.

The immediate objective was the town of Varna, on the Black Sea coast of Bulgaria. As usual, pandemonium broke out in the temporary camps at Scutari when the order to embark for Varna was given.

⊙ The quarter in which Lord Raglan lived seemed to be endowed with enormous centripetal and centrifugal forces, for generals, brigadiers, colonels of regiments, commissary officers and aides-de-camp were flying to and from them

* Now Istanbul

every moment of the day, as fast as their horses could carry them . . .

Sappers were busily engaged in fitting up horse-boxes on board the transports, all the stores required for the troops having been previously put on board.

The Sea of Marmara was covered with the white sails of transports and store ships making way against the current, and the little wharf and landing place at Scutari were alive with men working hard in loading boats with casks of provisions or munitions of war, while the air was shrill with the creaking and screaming of the wheels of buffalo carts toiling up and down the steep ascent to the barracks . . . ◉

That 'all the stores required for the troops' had not been loaded up was to become painfully obvious as time went by; partly because of their absence many men were to return to Scutari in appalling circumstances, and the little town was to become metaphorically and literally a stink in the nostrils. While describing its beach, somewhat surprisingly, as 'resembling that of Folkestone at high water', Russell gives a hint of the horrors to come:

◉ In the stagnant water which ripples almost imperceptibly on the shore there float all forms of nastiness and corruption, which the prowling dogs, standing leg-deep as they wade about in search of offal, cannot destroy.

The smell from the shore was noisome . . . the fringe of buoyant cats, dogs, birds, straw, sticks, in fact of all sorts of abominable flotsam and jetsam, bob about on the pebbles unceasingly. . . . The slaughter-houses for the troops, erected by the sea-side, did not contribute, as may readily be imagined, to the cleanliness of this filthy beach, or the wholesomeness of the atmosphere . . . ◉

This was the place to which, later on, the wounded, the sick and the dying were to be sent for hospitalisation.

One great concession was made to the Guards immediately before they embarked, as a curious form of celebration of the

Queen's birthday.

⊙ They were ordered to appear the following day on parade without: Muskets?—No. Coatees?—No. Epaulettes? —No. Cartouch-boxes?—No. Boots?—No. In fact her Majesty's Guards were actually commanded to parade WITH-OUT STOCKS! . . . and never since they were formed did the regiments give three more ringing, thundering cheers than issued from their throats on that occasion, when they marched on the ground as erect and upright as ever, but not 'caught by the windpipe', to be inspected by Lord Raglan. ⊙

What Russell does not mention—indeed perhaps he was not even aware of it at the time—was that the new freedom so much appreciated by the Guards was his own doing. The day after publication of his dispatch about Sir George Brown's mania for 'correct' dress, the then Secretary at War, Sidney Herbert, had announced a relaxation in 'the extreme formality of military uniform, including the abolition of the stock'. It was a small triumph, but one for which the men must have been heartily thankful.

The convoy for Varna sailed at the very end of May, in the evening. By the time it entered the Black Sea it was dark, and visibility rapidly became worse.

⊙ A fog, a drifting, clammy, nasty mist, bluish white and cold and raw, fell down upon us like a shroud, obscured the stars and all the lights of heaven and stole with a slug-like pace down yard and mast and stays, stuck to the face and beard, rendered the deck dark as a grave-yard . . . ⊙

Even so, they made port by the next evening and, with French assistance, camp was set up with a little less fuss than there had been at Gallipoli.

Even Russell managed to find somewhere to stay at nearby Aladyn and was given permission to draw rations for himself, a servant, and his horse. In spite of Delane's intervention he had received little help from the authorities in crossing to Varna; he was still not allowed to pitch a tent inside the

The Light Division Camp at Varna

lines, and so was completely without protection from robbery 'except what I can provide myself'.

Nevertheless his, as usual, minute description of the area makes it sound idyllic:

⊙ When the morning sun had risen it was scarcely possible for one to imagine himself far from England. At the other side of the lake which waters the meadows beneath the hill on which the camp was placed was a range of high ground finely wooded, with short crisp grass between the clumps of forest timber.

The open country was finely diversified, with abundance of wood and water all around. Long lines of storks flew overhead or held solemn reviews among the frogs in the meadows.

. . . Eagles soared . . . looking out for dead horses, and vultures, kites and huge buzzards scoured the plains in quest of vermin, hares or partridges.

Beautiful orioles, a blaze of green and yellow, gaudy woodpeckers, apiasters, jays and grosbeaks, shrieked and chattered among the bushes, while a lovely little warbler in a black cap and red waistcoat with bluish facings, darted about after the flies, and when he had caught and eaten one, lighted on a twig and expressed his satisfaction in a gush of exquisite music. ⊙

But there were discordant notes. Although the birds may have welcomed the army with joyous song (except for the dove, who was 'found so good to eat that his cooing was often abruptly terminated by a dose of No. 6'), there were swarms of insects, including fleas and enormous red ants which ravaged food supplies. In the undergrowth there were slugs, snakes and leeches. And everywhere there were terrible 'man-eating' flies which also attacked and maddened the horses so that their continual stamping and screaming kept the men awake at night.

The human inhabitants of the area were not very happy with their visitors either.

⊙ The people were so shy it was impossible to establish friendly relations with them. The inhabitants of Aladyn, close to the camp at the borders of the lake, abandoned their houses altogether. Not one living creature remained out of the 350 or 400 people who were there on our arrival. Their houses were left wide open, and such of their household goods as they could not remove, and a few cocks and hens that could not be caught, were all that was left behind.

The cause . . . for this exodus was the violence of a few ruffians on two or three occasions, coupled with groundless apprehension of the slaughter-house there. Certainly the smell was abominable. Diarrhœa broke out in the camp soon after my arrival and continued to haunt us all during the summer.

Much of this increase of disease must be attributed to the use of the red wine of the country, sold at the canteens of the camp; but as the men could get nothing else, they thought it was better to drink than the water of the place . . . ⊙

Once again the lack of supplies—this time of 'some wholesome drink (which) ought to have been provided to preserve the men from attacks of sickness in a climate where the heat was so great and the supply of pure water inadequate'—was to have grim consequences.

But Russell did not only carp and complain and criticise. He appreciated the problems and difficulties this wholly inexperienced army was up against, merely in its daily routine living.

⊙ No one unacquainted with the actual requirements of an army can form the smallest notion of the various duties which devolve upon a commissariat or of the enormous quantity of stores required for the daily use of man and horse.

At this very moment the quantity of food supplied for horses daily by the commissariat seems to a civilian almost fabulous, and, as it is all drawn from store at Varna, because the harvest is not yet thrashed in the country, the exertions of the officers charged with the supply are taxed to the uttermost to keep pace with the demand, so as to have a proper reserve.

What do you suppose the daily issue of rations for horses amounts to? To no less than 110,000 pounds weight of corn, chopped straw etc. 110,000 pounds! And this quantity will be increased day after day as horses come in from the country. Add to this about 27,000 lb rations of meat, 27,000 lb rations of bread, the same quantity of rice, tea, coffee, sugar etc. and it will be seen that the commissariat has enough on its hands.

But the issue and supply of rations is but a small portion of their duty. They have to provide horses, carts, saddles, packsaddles, tents, carriages for Dragoons, Light Cavalry, Infantry, Artillery, Sappers and Miners, and interpreters, and to provide the innumerable legitimate wants of an army in the field . . .

Large as our commissariat staff may appear, I can answer for it that they are worked to the very uttermost. Commissary-General Filder's office in Varna is like a bank in the City in the height of business, and the various officers at their desks are to be seen writing away as if their lives depended on it . . .

As the Bulgarian summer went on the heat intensified beyond anything the men had previously experienced. The inhabitants of Aladyn who had fled so precipitately before the hordes of (however friendly) invaders did not linger long enough to tell them that the beautiful valley in which they were encamped was known locally as 'the valley of death'.

In the light of the events which were to follow it seems likely that the vultures, kites and buzzards Russell wrote about so lyrically were on the look-out for bigger game than partridges or hares.

The Commissariat Camp in the Crimea, 3rd Division

4
The valley of death

June 1854. The expected advance of the Russians into
Bulgaria did not after all take place. The Turks were so
successful in their flank attacks that by mid-June the enemy
was in full retreat. When Lord Cardigan, Commander of the
famous Light Brigade, led a reconnaissance he 'found no sign
of the Russian army'. (His eyes were less sharp than the
Russians'—a contingent of them watched his Lordship's
cavalry 'riding up and down', from the opposite bank of the
Danube!)

The reconnaissance itself was a minor disaster. Lord
Cardigan was one of the wealthy young men who had bought
himself a regiment: the 11th Light Dragoons, picturesquely
nick-named 'Prince Albert's Own' since they attended the
Prince Consort on his arrival in England for his marriage to
Queen Victoria.

Nobody stopped him taking up this post, although he had
only two years previously been removed from the 15th
Hussars as 'unfit to command'. He had also been tried by his
peers in the House of Lords on a felony charge (having shot
and wounded a fellow officer in a duel) from which he
escaped only on a legal technicality.

He was a man of violent temper, popularly known as 'the
plague-spot of the British Army' and 'Jim the Bear'; an
arrogant bully, pitiless to junior officers and men serving
under him when they aroused his displeasure—which they
could do on the slightest grounds, or even no grounds at all.

A second unsuccessful attempt had already been made to

Lord Cardigan

remove him from his command of the 11th Hussars (also known as the 'cherry-pickers' because of the absurdly tight red pants they wore) after he had caused a man to be flogged on Easter Sunday morning, immediately following and in the same place as Divine Service had been held. No less a person than the Duke of Wellington saved him on that occasion.

He went to the Crimea with the rank of Brigadier-General and Commander of the Light Brigade, and in a highly dangerous mood. His brother-in-law, Lord Lucan—a man as arrogant and tyrannical as himself, with whom he was at daggers drawn—had been appointed overall Commander of the Cavalry Division, and so his superior in the field. From the time the appointments were made they ceased to be on speaking terms—not ideal conditions for fighting a war.

At first Lord Cardigan believed that, although officially

subordinate to his hated relative, he would operate the Light Brigade separately, and not be subject to Lord Lucan's orders. It was a fatal misunderstanding which was to add to the muddle and the massacre; not least because Lord Raglan, finding himself with such quarrelsome officers on his hands, did his level best to keep them apart—sometimes issuing orders direct to Lord Cardigan instead of through Lord Lucan.

On just such orders received directly from the Commander-in-Chief the reconnaissance party, magnificent in full regimentals, set off from Varna in search of the Russians.

After four days, as the sun was going down, a single horseman, exhausted and smothered in dust, rode slowly back into the camp, where his horse dramatically collapsed beneath him.

He brought disturbing news, 'that the squadrons will not return for some days; their fatigue has been excessive and hardships great—marching incessantly, for which neither men nor horses are fit . . .'

The patrol was in all away for two weeks, during which they slept rough, never once took off their clothes, and ate nothing but salt pork. On July 11th they came straggling back, mostly on foot, driving or leading their crippled horses. Nearly a hundred of the Light Brigade's best mounts were lost, Five horses died and seventy-five more were dying. The rest were in a sorry state. And this, without even engaging the enemy.

So far as Lord Cardigan was concerned, however, the expedition had been quite satisfactory. He was promoted Major-General.

Disappointed and nonplussed to find the Russians immediately beyond their reach, the British and French armies remained uneasily where they were. To carry the war forward it now became clear that an invasion of Russian soil would have to be made—and war-fever in England made it very clear that this was expected. *The Times* itself insisted.

'. . . The grand political and military objects of the war cannot be attained so long as Sebastopol and the Russian Fleet are in existence . . .' (It was of course from Sebastopol that the Russian squadron had sailed to sink the Turkish flotilla.)

The trouble was that the Commanders, like everyone else, were completely ignorant of this part of the world and had no idea how to set about such an invasion. They had no knowledge even of the climate, which was alternately to freeze and fry them, nor of the unseen dangers which could, with better organisation, have been avoided.

The result was that long before they came to grips with the Russians they were at war with a very different, and terrifying, enemy—cholera.

Surprisingly, in spite of its better organisation, it was the French army which was first devastated by the disease. In the early stages the British remained comparatively free. But their luck was not to last.

July 1854. Russell, now at last living in camp with the Light Division, went down to Varna on July 20th to 'get some articles of outfit'.

◉ Up to this time there had been no case of cholera in the Light Division; but early on Sunday morning, 23rd, it broke out with the same extraordinary violence and fatal effect which has marked its appearance in the French columns, and the camp was further broken up forthwith and the men marched to Monastir, nine miles further on towards the Balkans.

In Varna the inhabitants suffered from the pestilence as much as the troops. Many of them fled from the town and encamped near the neighbouring villages. Turks and Greeks suffered alike, and perished 'like flies' to use their own image. ◉

Two missions set off about this time to explore the possibilities for following up the Turkish defeat of the Russians. H.M.S. *Fury*, with high-ranking British and French officers on board, went off in great secrecy to explore the coast of the Crimean peninsula—a near-island jutting south into the Black Sea from the Russian mainland, with Sebastopol at its south-western tip. And a French expedition set off northwards by land to where it was rumoured ten thousand Russians lurked.

This second expedition had several aims: to raise morale, to remove the troops from the camps already devastated by cholera, and, almost incidentally, to strike a blow at the Russians before the 'serious' attacks on the Crimea began.

The French 1st Division arrived at Constanta, north of Varna on the Black Sea coast, on July 28th.

⊚ . . . They found that the whole country had been laid waste by fire and sword—the towns and villages burnt and destroyed, the stock and crops carried off.

On that night, just ere the French broke up their camp in order to set out on this march, the cholera declared itself among them with an extraordinary and dreadful violence. Between midnight and eight o'clock next morning nearly 600 men lay dead in their tents. At the same moment the division of Espinasse was stricken with equal rapidity and violence at Kerjelouk.

All that night men suffered and died, and on the 31st July General Yusuf made his appearance at Kostendji with the remains of his haggard and horror-stricken troops and proceeded towards Mangalia in his death-march.

On the 1st August General Canrobert, who had returned from his reconnaissance,* arrived at Constanta from Varna and was horrified to find that his camp was but a miserable hospital, where the living could scarcely bury the remains of their comrades. He could pity and could suffer, but he could not save.

* To the Crimean peninsula, on board H.M.S. *Fury*

That day and the next the pestilence redoubled in intensity, and in the midst of all these horrors food fell short . . .

The 2nd and 3rd Divisions were also afflicted by the same terrible scourge and there was nothing left for the Generals but to lead their man back to their encampments as soon as they could, leaving behind them the dead and the dying. ⊙

The troops returned to find 'the same awful plague developing with increasing strength and vigour' in Varna. Fear, almost as demoralising as the disease itself, swept through the camps.

Meanwhile, the 'secret' mission to the Crimea had returned with, at last, some useful information. Eupatoria, forty miles north of the fortified port of Sebastopol, was the spot noted as a possible landing place.

Between it and the armies' ultimate objective, the port itself, there were four rivers to cross: the Alma, the Katscha, the Belbeck and the Tchernaya—and between them four ranges of hills of varying heights and steepness.

Desire to escape from 'the valley of death' speeded the operation, which in the circumstances was horrifyingly risky. Disorganised as they were to begin with, and adding the confusion and weakness caused by the ravages of disease, the British and French armies were in no shape, as had been shown by Lord Cardigan's brief foray and the French reconnaissance north to Constanta, for any sort of sustained attack on an army of unknown strength (but probably vastly greater than their own) in unknown territory.

Another worry was engaging the minds of the Commanders, though. Summer in the Black Sea area was bad enough, but winter lay ahead and that might be infinitely worse. It was a choice between evils; and of the two the immediate evil seemed the greater.

⊙ The French losses from cholera were frightful. Convinced that there was something radically wrong in the air of the hospital at Varna, the French cleared out of the building altogether, and resolved to treat their cases in the field.

The hospital had been formerly used as a Turkish barrack. It was a huge quadrangular building, like the barracks at Scutari, with a courtyard in the centre. The sides of the square were about 150 feet long, and each of them contained three floors, consisting of spacious corridors, with numerous rooms off them . . . About one-third of the building was reserved for our use; the remainder was occupied by the French.

Although not very old, the building was far from being in thorough repair. The windows were broken, the walls in parts were cracked and shaky, and the floors were mouldering and rotten. Like all places which have been inhabited by Turkish soldiers for any time, the smell of the buildings was abominable. Men sent in there with fevers and other disorders were frequently attacked with the cholera in its worst form and died with unusual rapidity, in spite of all that could be done to save them.

I visited the hospital and observed that a long train of carts filled with sick soldiers were drawn up by the walls. There were thirty-five carts, with three or four men in each. These were sick French soldiers sent in from the camps and waiting till room could be found for them in the hospital.

A number of soldiers were sitting down by the roadside and here and there the moonbeams flashed brightly off their piled arms. The men were silent; not a song, not a laugh. A gloom, seldom seen among French troops, reigned amid these groups of grey-coated men and the quiet that prevailed was only broken now and then by the moans and cries of the poor sufferers in the carts.

Observing that about fifteen arabas without any occupants were waiting in the square, I asked a *sous-officier* for what purpose they were required. His answer, sullen and short, was 'For the dead . . . Monsieur'.

The white walls of the fatal hospital looked clean and neat

as they towered above the lengthened *cortège* of the dead which lay in deep shadow at its base, but the murmurings of sickness and the groans of the dying stole out on the night air through the long lines of latticed windows.

As I turned away and spurred under the gateway which leads to the English quarter, I encountered a burial party escorting the bodies of six of our own poor fellows to their last resting-place, outside the walls by the sea beach of Varna . . .

In the hospital itself I observed a great deal of confusion and want of method, or, at least, an appearance of over-work on the part of officers and men which made them seem surly and indifferent. Indeed, I heard one of the hospital orderlies say he had not been in bed for fifty-six hours, and had had no sleep for twenty-four hours . . . the surgical staff . . . are penned up, two or three together, in small unfurnished rooms, open to every wind that blows through wall, floor, ceiling and window. Some of these gentlemen have no rooms at all, and one I know sleeps in a passage . . . ◉

August 1854. Disillusion was creeping more and more into Russell's reports now: disillusion not only with the British army's incompetence, the French army's superiority, but with the very people both armies had come to help—the Turks. The condition of buildings taken over by the British and French from the Turkish army was nauseous, dirty and verminous. It was, Russell comments with startling honesty:

◉ . . . a great pity that it is not permitted to us to hate the Turks and Turkey; certainly it is done to a vast extent without permission, by the British army.

The bravery of the Turks we admire and respect, their indomitable courage in defence of their country, or rather in defence of the boundaries of their empire, we applaud and wonder at; but their manners and customs, their physical peculiarities and their tastes, we can neither appreciate nor endure . . . ◉

Quarrels broke out between the different nationalities. There was fighting. Disaster piled on disaster.

◉ On the night of August 10th a great fire broke out at Varna which utterly destroyed more than a quarter of the town. The sailors of the ships, and the French and English soldiery stationed near the town, worked with the greatest energy for the ten hours during which the fire lasted; but as a brisk wind prevailed, which fanned the flames as they leapt along the wooden streets, their efforts were not as successful as they deserved.

The fire broke out near the French commissariat stores, in the spirit shop. The officers in charge broached many casks of spirits and as the liquid ran down the streets a Greek was seen to set fire to it. He was cut down to the chin by a French officer and fell into the fiery torrent.

The howling of the inhabitants, the yells of the Turks, the clamour of the women, children, dogs and horses, were appalling.

Marshal St Arnaud* displayed great vigour and coolness in superintending the operations of the troops, and by his exertions aggravated the symptoms of the malady from which he had long been suffering.

The French lost great quantities of provisions, and we had many thousand rations of biscuits utterly consumed. In addition, immense quantities of stores were destroyed— 19,000 pairs of soldiers' shoes and an immense quantity of cavalry sabres, which were found amid the ruins fused into the most fantastic shapes.

To add to our misfortunes the cholera broke out in the fleets in Varna Bay and at Baltschik with extraordinary virulence. The *Friedland* and *Montebello* suffered in particular—in the latter upwards of 100 died in twenty-four

* Commander-in-Chief of the French Forces at that time

hours.

The conduct of many of the men, French and English, seemed characterised by a recklessness verging on insanity. They might be seen lying drunk in the kennels, or in the ditches by the road-sides, under the blazing rays of the sun, covered with swarms of flies. They might be seen in stupid sobriety gravely paring the rind off cucumbers of portentous dimensions and eating the deadly cylinders one after another to the number of six or eight, till there was no room for more; or frequently three or four of them would make a happy bargain with a Greek for a large basketful of apricots, scarlet pumpkins, water melons, wooden-bodied pears, green-gages and plums, and then retire beneath the shade of a tree, where they divided and ate the luscious food till nought remained but a heap of peel, rind and stones.

They then diluted the mass of fruit with raki, or peach brandy, and would straggle home or to sleep as best they could. It was no wonder indeed that cholera throve and fattened among us. In the second week in August it assumed such an alarming character that both Admirals . . . resolved to leave their anchorage and stand out to sea for a cruise . . .

On Wednesday the 16th, the *Caradoc* which left Constantinople with the mails for the fleet and army the previous evening, came up with the English fleet . . . and the appalling intelligence that the flag-ship had lost seventy men since she left Baltschik and that she had buried ten men that morning. Upwards of 100 men were on the sick list . . . ☉

The great fire of Varna had one beneficial effect, not unlike that of the Great Fire of London which followed the Great Plague of 1665:

☉ . . . the cholera seemed to diminish in the town itself and the reports from the various camps were much more favourable than before . . . ☉

The British army was now scattered widely around the

countryside, from Monastir to Varna: 'a distance of 26 or 27 miles'. Too late it was discovered that:

⊙ . . . notwithstanding the exquisite beauty of the country around Aladyn, it was a hot-bed of fever and dysentery. The same was true of Devno, which was called by the Turks 'The Valley of Death' . . . Had we consulted the natives ere we pitched our camps, we assuredly should never have gone either to Aladyn or Devno, notwithstanding the charms of their position and the temptations offered by the abundant supply of water and by the adjacent woods . . .

Whoever gazed on the rich meadows, stretching for long miles away, and bordered by heights on which dense forests struggled all but in vain to pierce the masses of wild vine, clematis, dwarf acacia and many-coloured brushwoods, might well have imagined that no English glade or hill-top could be healthier or better suited for the residence of man. But those meadows nurtured the fever, the ague, dysentery and pestilence in their bosom—the lake and the stream exhaled death, and at night fat unctuous vapours rose fold after fold from the valleys and crept up in the dark and stole into the tent of the sleeper and wrapped him in their deadly embrace.

So completely exhausted was the Brigade of Guards after a short encampment that 3,000 of the flower of England had to make two marches in order to get over the distance from Aladyn to Varna, which was not more than ten miles . . .

But that was not all. Their packs were carried for them. Just think of this, good people of England, who are sitting anxiously in your homes, day after day, expecting every morning to gladden your eyes with the sight of the announcement in large type of 'Fall of Sebastopol'—your Guards, your *corps d'élite*, the pride of your hearts, and the delight of your eyes . . . whose stature, strength, and massive bulk you exhibit to kingly visitors as no inapt symbols of your nation, have been so reduced by sickness, disease, and a depressing climate, that it was judged inexpedient to allow them to carry their own packs, or to permit them to march more than five miles a day . . .

Think of this, and then judge whether these men are fit in their present state to go to Sebastopol, or to attempt any great operation of war . . . ◉

Every section of the army had been decimated. Even the ambulance corps was crippled. Physically and morally each division of the army had been weakened by nearly one regiment.

Russell was worried not only by the decimation of the army, but its demoralisation.

◉ I am certain steps ought to be taken to stimulate the spirits of the men. They 'sup full of horrors', and listen greedily to tales of death which serve but to weaken and terrify them. The sound of the cannon and the sight of the Russians would do more to rouse them from this gloomy mood than all the 'doctor's stuff', as the men term medicine, or change of air in the world. ◉

Certainly nothing they were to experience in battle was likely to be worse than what surrounded them now.

Of the French 'cholera camp' two miles outside the town, Russell wrote:

◉ Horrors occurred here every day which were shocking to think of. Walking by the beach one might see some straw sticking up through the sand, and on scraping it away . . . be horrified at bringing to light the face of a corpse which had been deposited there with a wisp of straw around it, a prey to dogs and vultures.

Dead bodies rose from the bottom in the harbour and bobbed grimly around in the water or floated in from sea and drifted past the sickened gazers on board the ships—all buoyant, bolt upright and hideous in the sun.

One day, the body of a French soldier who had been murdered (for his neckerchief was twisted round the neck so as to produce strangulation, and the forehead was laid open by a ghastly wound which cleft the skull to the brain), came alongside the *Caradoc* in harbour and was with difficulty sunk again. ◉

Yes, it was more than obviously time to get away from the area which had seen so much suffering. Time, too, for some action to take the men's minds off the hideous sights, and sounds, and smells, which had surrounded them for far too long.

5

Old generals, young lords and tentless soldiers

September 1854. All over London as the early morning sunshine streamed through lace curtains on to crisp white tablecloths, gentlemen with mutton-chop whiskers, soberly dressed in frock coats, high stiff collars and starched cuffs, shook out their copies of *The Times* and turned to the page giving news of 'The War in the East'.

◉ The daybreak of Thursday [September 14th] gave promise of a lovely morning . . .

The vast armada which had moved on during the night in perfect order, studding the horizon with a second heaven of stars, and covering the face of the sea with innumerable lights, advanced parallel with the coast till it gradually closed in towards the shore . . .

At seven a.m. most of the fleet were inshore . . . ◉

It all sounded incredibly easy. Sunlight on the water, the ships steaming peacefully into what appeared to be almost a

The English Army landing at Calamita Bay

tourist resort; flocks of wildfowl, farmhouses, clumps of aromatic herbs, the occasional farm cart bowling along a narrow road. Russell even spotted the Post Carriage from Sebastopol to Odessa 'rolling leisurely along, and conveying, probably, news of the great armament with which the coast was menaced'.

There was no sign of opposition, except for a party of Cossacks lurking just below the skyline. One thing Russell did not mention, however, was the sinister name of the landing place: Calamita Bay!

As might have been expected, the French were first to set foot on Russian soil. Within an hour of dropping anchor they had begun mass-landings. Within a second hour, 6,000 were on shore.

In all, Russell reports, 23,600 French soldiers and 27,000 British set foot on the beach before Eupatoria that morning.

⊙ The instant the French had landed a regiment, a company was pushed on to reconnoitre. As each regiment followed in column, its predecessors deployed and advanced in light marching order . . . spreading out like a fan over the plains . . . In about an hour after their first detachment had landed their advanced posts were discernible between three and four miles from the beach, like little black specks moving over the corn-fields, and darkening the highways and meadow-paths . . .

By twelve o'clock that barren and desolate beach, inhabited but a short time before only by seagull and wild-fowl, was swarming with life. From one extremity to the other, bayonets glistened and red coats and brass-mounted shakoes gleamed in solid masses. The air was filled with our English speech and the hum of voices mingled with loud notes of command.

Very amusing it was to watch the loading and unloading of the boats. A gig or cutter, pulled by eight or twelve sailors, with a paddle-box boat, flat or Turkish pinnace in tow would come up alongside the steamer or transport. . . . The officers of each company first descended, each man in full dress.

Over his shoulder was slung his haversack, containing what had been ere it underwent the process of cooking four pounds and a half of salt meat, and a bulky mass of biscuit of the same weight. This was his ration for three days. Besides this, each officer carried his greatcoat, rolled up and fastened in a hoop round his body, a wooden canteen to hold water, a small ration of spirits, whatever change of underclothing he could manage to stow away, his forage-cap, and in most instances, a revolver.

Each private carried his blanket and greatcoat strapped up into a kind of knapsack, inside which was a pair of boots, a pair of socks, a shirt, and at the request of the men themselves, a forage-cap; he also carried his water canteen, and the same rations as the officer, a portion of the mess cooking apparatus, firelock and bayonet of course, cartouch-box and fifty rounds of ball-cartridge for Minié, sixty rounds for smooth-bore arms.

As each man came creeping down the ladder, Jack helped him along tenderly from rung to rung till he was safe in the boat, took his firelock and stowed it away, removed his knapsack and packed it snugly under the seat, patted him on the back and told him 'not to be afeered on the water'; treated 'the sojer' in fact in a very kind and tender way as though he were a large but not very sagacious pet, who was not to be frightened or lost sight of on any account; and did it all so quickly that the large paddle-box boats, containing 100 men, were filled in five minutes.

Then the latter took the paddle-box in tow, leaving her, however, in charge of a careful coxswain, and the same attention was paid to getting the 'sojer' on shore that was evinced in getting him into the boat; the sailors (half or wholly naked in the surf) standing by at the bows and handing each man and his accoutrement down the plank to the shingle for fear 'he'd fall off and hurt himself'. ◉

The 'sojers' needed all the help they could get. It had been a grim crossing of the Black Sea. Some had been on board as long as seventeen days, for the last five of which they existed on salt pork and biscuits. There was a water shortage, and the spectre of cholera continued to hang over the sadly-depleted army.

As for the horses—words are inadequate to describe the conditions they endured throughout the voyage. Seventy-five more of them—the lucky ones perhaps—died before landfall was made.

Now they were—most of them—at last ashore . . . in enemy country, facing a huge army who knew that country like the proverbial backs of their hands and who, moreover, were fighting to defend their native land whereas the British and French hardly knew why they were there.

The British had little transport, practically no food and no ambulances for the sick and wounded; and though there were as yet no wounded there was still a vast number of sick.

◉ Many of the staff-officers, who ought to have been mounted, marched on foot, as their horses were not yet landed. Generals might be seen sitting on powder barrels on the beach, awaiting the arrival of 'divisional Staff horses' or retiring gloomily within the folds of their mackintosh.

Disconsolate doctors too were there, groaning after hospital panniers—but too sorely needed, for more than one man died on the beach. During the voyage several cases of cholera occurred: 150 men were buried on the passage from Varna, and there were about 300 men on board not able to move when we landed.

The beach was partitioned by flagstaffs with colours corresponding to that of each division . . . but it was, of course, almost beyond the limits of possibility to observe these nice distinctions in conducting an operation which must have extended over many square miles of water. ◉

Even the lovely morning was not to fulfil its promise.

◉ Few of those who were with the expedition will forget the night of the 14th September. Seldom or never were 27,000 Englishmen more miserable. No tents had been sent on shore, partly because there had been no time to land them, partly because there was no certainty of our being able to find carriage for them in case of a move.

Towards night the sky looked very black and lowering; the wind rose, and the rain fell in torrents. The showers increased about midnight and early in the morning fell in drenching sheets which pierced through the blankets and great-coats of the houseless and tentless soldiers. Imagine some of these old generals and young lords and gentlemen, exposed hour after hour to the violence of pitiless storms, with no bed but the reeking puddle under the saturated blankets, or bits of useless water-proof wrappers, and the twenty-odd thousand poor fellows who could not get 'dry bits' of ground, and had to sleep, or try to sleep, in little lochs and water-courses—no fire to cheer them, no hot grog, and the prospect of no breakfast.

Imagine this, and add to it that the 'nice change of linen' had become a wet abomination, which weighed the poor men's kits down, and . . . admit that this 'seasoning' was of a rather violent character . . . ◉

Russell wrote from the bitterest of personal experience. That night he himself lay under a cart, amongst the 'old generals, young lords and tentless soldiers', sleeping intermittently, listening to the beat of the surf on the beach, the steady drumming of the rain, and, echoing faintly and eerily across the water, the 'tang' of ship's bells.

◉ In one respect [he went on] the rain was of service; it gave the men a temporary supply of water—but then it put a fire out of the question, even if enough wood could have been scraped together to make it. The country was, however, quite destitute of timber.

During the night it blew freshly from the west, a heavy sea tumbled into the bay and sent a high surf upon the beach, which much interfered with the process of landing cavalry and artillery on the 15th.

Several valuable animals were drowned in an attempt to land some staff horses. Lord Raglan lost one charger, and another swam off seaward and was only recovered miles from the shore.

Some boats were staved and rendered useless, and several others were injured by the roll of the surf on the beach; nor did the horse boats and flats escape uninjured . . .

Before the disembarkation had concluded for the day, signal was made for all ships to 'land tents'. Subsequently the order was countermanded and the tents which had been landed were sent back to the ships again . . .

Our French allies, deficient as they have been in means of accommodation and stowage and transport, had yet managed to land their little scraps of tents the day they disembarked; whilst our poor fellows were soaked through and through, their blankets and greatcoats saturated with wet, and without a change of raiment, the French close at hand, and the Turks, whose tents were much more bulky than our own, were lying snugly under cover.

The most serious result of the wetting was . . . a great increase in illness among the troops. ⊙

The next two days, during which the burning sunshine returned to dry up not only the saturated blankets, but drinking water too, were spent in trying to sort out the muddle. Astonishingly, the Russians made no move to drive the expedition away. Parties of Cossacks were seen watching and making notes of the numbers and activities of the British and French; and at night a lurid glow in the sky inland spoke of 'scorched earth'—villages and crops being burned, as they had been in Bulgaria, to prevent anything useful falling into the hands of the invaders as the Russians retreated towards the stronghold of Sebastopol.

Lord Cardigan led one more disastrous and unproductive expedition to bring in information and supplies, returning once more empty-handed and with both men and horses in a state of collapse.

Then, on September 17th, news arrived that 15,000 Russians were assembled twelve miles south of the allied camp, on the River Alma.

⊙ At three o'clock in the morning the camp was roused by the reveille, and the 50,000 sleepers woke into active life . . . The English commissariat officers struggled in vain with the very deficient means at their disposal to meet the enormous requirements of an army of 26,000 men for the transport of baggage, ammunition and food; and a scene, which to an unpractised eye seemed one of utter confusion, began and continued for several hours, relieved only by the steadiness and order of the regiments as they paraded previous to marching.

The French, in advance on our right, were up betimes, and the camp fires of the allied armies, extending for miles along the horizon, and mingling with the lights of the ships, almost anticipated morning.

Six thousand Turkish infantry, under Suleiman Pasha, moved along by the sea-side; next to them came the divisions of Generals Bosquet, Canrobert, Forey and Prince Napoleon. Our order of march was about four miles to the left of their left wing, and as many behind them.

The right of the allied forces was covered by the fleet, which moved along with it in magnificent order, darkening the air with innumerable columns of smoke, ready to shell the enemy should they threaten to attack our right and commanding the land for nearly two miles from the shore.

It was nine o'clock in the morning ere the whole of our army was ready for marching. The day was warm, and our advance was delayed by the wretched transport furnished for the baggage, an evil which even at that time threatened to be more severely felt in any protracted operations. Everything not absolutely indispensable was sent on board ship. At last the men fell in and the march of the campaign began . . .

After a march of an hour a halt took place for fifty minutes, during which Lord Raglan, accompanied by a very large staff, Marshal St Arnaud and a number of French officers, rode along the front of the columns. The men of their own accord got up from the ground, rushed forward, and column after column rent the air with three thundering English cheers. It was a good omen.

The troops presented a splendid appearance. The effect of

these grand masses of soldiery descending the ridges of the hills, rank after rank, with the sun playing over forests of glittering steel, can never be forgotten by those who witnessed it.

At last, the smoke of burning villages and farmhouses announced that the enemy in front were aware of our march. It was melancholy to see the white walls of the houses blackened with smoke—the flames ascending through the roofs of peaceful homesteads—and the ruined outlines of deserted hamlets.

Many sick men fell out and were carried to the rear. It was a painful sight—a sad contrast to the magnificent appearance of the army in front, to behold litter after litter borne past to the carts with the poor sufferers who had dropped from illness and fatigue. ◉

Already the troops were within thirty miles of the fortress-town of Sebastopol which was their objective, and the only shots fired were a few on landing, one of which had wounded a little araba-boy. The Russians, it seemed, were giving the allied armies plenty of rope, devastating the countryside as they retreated further and further from the landing place at Calamita Bay. Then, suddenly, they were in sight . . .

◉ . . . from the top of a hill, a wide plain was visible, beyond which rose a ridge darkened here and there by masses which the practised eye recognised as cavalry. On the left . . . lay a large village in flames; right before us a neat white house unburnt, though the out-houses and farmyard were burning. This was the Imperial Post-house of Bouljanak.

The house was deserted and gutted. Only a picture of a saint, bunches of herbs in the kitchen, and a few household utensils were left; and a solitary pea-hen stalked sadly about the threshold, which soon fell victim to a revolver.

A small stream (the Bouljanak) ran past us, which was an object of delight to our thirsty soldiers who had marched more than eight miles from their late camp . . . (Lack of water was a permanent problem in this country, not helped by the fact that the chief item of diet was salt pork.)

After a short halt . . . the army pushed on again . . . and on arriving about a mile beyond the post-house we clearly made out the Cossack Lancers on the hills in front.

Lord Cardigan threw out skirmishers in line, who covered the front at intervals of ten or twelve yards from each other. The Cossacks advanced to meet us in like order, man for man, the steel of their long lances glittering in the sun. They were rough-looking fellows, mounted on sturdy little horses; but the regularity of their order and the celerity of their movements showed that they were regulars and by no means despicable foes . . .

Lord Cardigan was eager to try their strength and permission was given to him to advance somewhat nearer; but as he did so, dark columns of cavalry appeared in the recesses of the hills, and it became evident that if our men charged up such a steep ascent their horses would be blown, and they would run a risk of being surrounded and cut to pieces by a force three times their number. Lord Lucan therefore ordered the cavalry to halt, gather in their skirmishers, and retire slowly . . .

When our skirmishers halted, the Cossacks commenced a fire of carabines from their line of vedettes, which was quite harmless. Few of the balls came near enough to let the whizz be heard. I was riding between the cavalry and the skirmishers, with Lieutenant Colonel Dickson R.A., when suddenly the Russians, emboldened by our halt, came over the brow of the hill, and slowly descended the slope in three solid squares, the centre one of which advanced nearer than the others.

'Now,' said Dickson, 'we'll catch it. These fellows have guns and mean mischief.'

I, in my ignorance, conceived that it would be a very

pleasant thing to look at, whatever they meant. We had offered them battle, and they had lost their chance, for our cavalry now turned round and rode quietly towards the troops . . .

At every fifty paces our cavalry faced about to receive the Cossacks if they prepared to charge. Suddenly one of the Russian cavalry squares opened: a spirt [sic] of white smoke rose out of the gap and round shot, which first pitched close to my horse and covered me with dirt, tore over the column of our cavalry behind and rolled away between the ranks of the riflemen in the rear just as they came in view of the cavalry.

In another instant a second shot knocked over a horse, taking off his rider's leg above the ankle. Another and another followed, tearing through our ranks.

All this time our cavalry were drawn up as targets for the enemy's guns, and had they been of iron they could not have been more solid and immovable. The Russian gunners fired admirably; they were rather slow, but their balls came bounding along, quite visible as they passed . . . ◉

The British artillery opened fire in reply to the Russian guns, and after a short, sharp exchange the Russians retired.

◉ It is impossible to form an accurate notion of the effect of our fire, but it must have caused the Russians a greater loss than they inflicted upon us. We lost six horses and four men were wounded.

One of the wounded men rode coolly to the rear with his foot dangling by a piece of skin to the bone and told the doctor he had just come to have his leg dressed. Another wounded trooper behaved with equal fortitude and refused the use of a litter to carry him to the rear, though his leg was broken into splinters . . .

When the Russians had retired beyond the heights, orders were given to halt and bivouac for the night, and our tired men set to work to gather fuel. So ended the affair of the Bouljanak . . .

As soon as the rations of rum and meat had been served out, the casks were broken up and the staves used to make fires for cooking, aided by nettles and long grass.

At night the watch-fires of the Russians were visible on our left and front. It was cold and dreary and if I could intrude the recital of the sorrows of a tentless, baggage-less man wandering about in the dark from regiment to regiment in hope of finding his missing traps (which were thrown out of the commissariat araba in which they had been placed, by order of the Commissariat General . . . I never saw them again . . .) I might tell a tale amusing enough to read, the incidents of which were very distressing to the individual concerned.

The night was damp, the watch-fires were mere flashes, which gave little heat, and barely sufficed to warm the rations; but the wanderer was lucky enough to get a lodging on the ground beside a kindly colonel, who was fortunate enough to have a little field-tent with him, and a bit of bread and biscuit to spare after a march of ten miles and a fast of ten hours. ◉

So ended Russell's Crimean baptism of fire, and the allies' first less-than-satisfactory encounter with the Russian army.

6
Scarlet poppies (The Battle of the Alma)

September 20th, 1854, a date to be written in British history books as 'The Battle of the Alma'.

In the cold pre-dawn which heralded a beautiful morning

the watch-fires had at last winked out. Men lay sprawled,
or huddled, exhausted, under their great-coats.

Some muttered and whimpered, twitching in feverish sleep.
Some lay so still it was clear they would never move again.
As the sun rose to dry out the dew, comrades hardly fitter
than themselves dragged or carried them shorewards, to be
taken aboard the ships standing out, or for burial. There was
no time, and no one, to care for the sick and dying now—for
beyond the peaceful meadows and vineyards, and beyond the
shallow waters of the Alma river, poised on the vantage point
of a high plateau, the Russian army silently waited, its guns
trained on the bridges, the fords, and the steep, unwelcoming
slopes up which the allies must scramble to face them . . .
if they ever got so far.

As usual, the operation began with muddle, confusion,
misunderstanding, recrimination, insufficient reconnaissance
and lack of communication.

The British, to reach their battle position, were faced with
a two-and-a-half-hour march, a bad start for men who,
despite Russell's enthusiasm for their appearance, were falling 'like scarlet poppies', convulsed with dysentery, cholera
and heat-stroke; half-maddened by thirst, hollow-eyed from
lack of proper food and sleep.

About ten o'clock the British line finally moved towards
the Alma; and in spite of the suffering, the sickness and the
dying, a feverish atmosphere curiously like that of a school
sports-day persisted.

◉ . . . when the regiments halted (to gather up our rear)
I went through the Light Division, part of the 2nd Division,
the Guards and the Highlanders. I found all my friends, save
one or two, in high spirits. Some had received letters from
wives and children by the mail, which made them look grave
and think seriously on the struggle to come. Others were
joking and laughing in the best possible spirits. Many a
laugh did I hear from lips which in two hours more were

closed for ever.

The officers and men made the most of this delay and ate whatever they had with them; but there was a great want of water, and the salt pork made them so thirsty that in the subsequent passage of the Alma, under the heaviest fire, the men stopped to drink and to fill their water canteens . . . ◉

Russell himself must have cut a curious figure. Never having been able satisfactorily to replace the gear he lost in Malta he now wore a Commissariat officer's cap with a broad gold band, a rifleman's patrol jacket, cord breeches, butcher boots and huge spurs. The previous day he had been peremptorily halted by an officer:

'General Pennefather wants to know who you are, sir, and what you are doing here.'

When Russell attempted to explain his presence he was asked to report direct to the General. He did so, as best he could.

'By——, Sir,' the General exploded, 'I had as soon see the devil! What do you know about this kind of work, and what

Cartoon—'Landing of our own *Times* Correspondent and destruction of the other Correspondents' (Sketch by Captain Swaeby)

will you do when we get into action?'

Russell was not easily put out. 'Well, Sir,' he slyly replied, 'it is quite true I have very little acquaintance with the business, but I suspect there are a great many here with no greater knowledge than myself.'

The General, disarmed, threw back his head and laughed. 'Begad, you're right,' he admitted, and after a little further conversation advised Russell to 'keep away from the front if you don't want to have you nose cut short'.

It was a reminder to Russell—if by now he needed it!—that he had no official position, or even right, to be where he was; and the uncertainty as to his status was reinforced when the Commander of the 2nd Division approached him with a similar query, and when told that Russell had made no 'arrangements' to accompany the army turned on him sternly.

'You do not know what you are about. Nor do those who sent you understand what they are doing. Do get attached to something or other. You must go to the Commissary General, to the Chaplain-in-Chief—to anyone you know. Get attached to something . . .'

The next day, as the advance on the Alma began, he tacked himself as unobtrusively as possible on to the Commander-in-Chief's cavalcade, but he was not an unobtrusive man, and again he was chivied by the A.D.C. to the Superintendent of Royal Engineers with the petulant words, 'I'll send Sir John to you, I will, if you don't go . . .'

⊙ I never was [Russell reported] in a more unpleasant position. Everyone else on the field had some reason for being there. I had none. They were on recognised business. It could scarcely be a recognised or legitimate business for any man to ride in front of the Army in order that he might be able to write an account of a battle for a newspaper. I was a very fly in amber. ⊙

He was suddenly, and forcibly, reminded of another aspect

77

of his unofficial presence when he came across an officer reading a letter from his wife, which had arrived that morning in the mail-delivery from one of the ships standing offshore.

'Well, thank God,' the officer remarked with a sigh as he tucked the letter away, 'she'll have something more than her widow's pension if I am knocked on the head to-day.'

'No pension for *my* widow if *I* fall,' Russell thought, with something of a shock, 'and for myself the motto: "Served him right." Very true, but very late to occur to me!'

(In fact only a few weeks later Russell received a letter from John Walter, proprietor of *The Times*, to say that he had invested five hundred pounds in trust for the benefit of Russell's children.)

One more problem confronted Russell at this, his first real battle. He could, being merely mortal, see only one aspect of it, and had no way of knowing where his best vantage point might be. Yet it was important for him to get the best overall view, since his report would be the one which gave readers of 'the world's best newspaper' their immediate, and possibly life-long, impression of events as they occurred.

It was obvious he could not rely on help from army staff, who had already ordered him from the battlefield. As the battle progressed the problem became intensified by his own personal reactions.

⊙ How was I to describe what I had not seen? Where learn the facts for which they were waiting at home? My eyes swam as I tried to make notes of what I heard. I was worn out with excitement, fatigue, and want of food. I had been more than ten hours in the saddle; my wretched horse, bleeding badly from a cut in the leg, was unable to carry me. My head throbbed, my heart beat as though it would burst.

I suppose I was unnerved by want of food and rest, but I was so much overcome by what I saw that I could not remain where the fight had been closest and deadliest. I

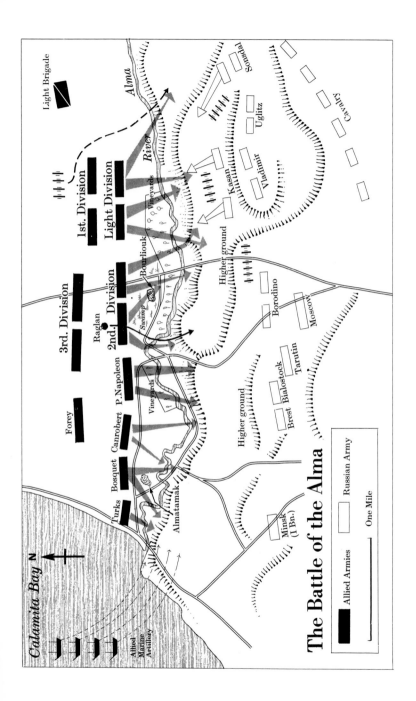

The Battle of the Alma

longed to get away from it—from the exultation of others in which thought for the dead was forgotten or unexpressed.

It was now that the weight of the task I had accepted fell on my soul like lead. ⊙

He was obviously in no state to write an impartial dispatch immediately, but conditions, and the closeness of the horror of the fighting, made sleep that night elusive and he woke next morning with a blinding headache. The crowded tent he shared with some of the officers was suffocatingly hot, and outside and inside the smell was sickening.

But the dispatch had to be written. Two officers, seeing him perched uncomfortably on the parapet of a battery, made a writing table for him from a plank laid on two casks. This first, perhaps confused, account of the Battle of the Alma never reached London and Russell was thankful for it. After it was written he borrowed a horse and set out to collect more information. Then he wrote a second report. It was as straightforward and accurate as he could make it. Later he commented:

⊙ I did not then grasp the fact that I had it in my power to give a halo of glory to some unknown warrior by putting his name in type. Indeed, for many a month I never understood that particular attribute of my unfortunate position, and I may say now in all sincerity and truth, I never knowingly made use of it. ⊙

Russell began his revised dispatch by describing the plan of attack, and the terrain over which the battle was to be fought. Then he continued:

⊙ . . . I joined the general staff and for some time rode with them.

There was at the time very little to be seen and there were so many officers with Lord Raglan that it was difficult to see in front at all; so observing Sir de Lacy Evans (Commander of the 2nd Division) on higher ground about a quarter of a mile away, I turned my horse to join him. An instant afterwards a round shot rushed over the heads of the staff, being fired at the Rifles in advance of them.

By the time I had reached Sir de Lacy the round shot were rolling through the columns, and the men halted and lay down by order of Lord Raglan. Sir de Lacy said, 'Well, if you want to see a great battle, you're in a fair way of having your wish gratified.'

At this moment the whole of the village in our front burst into flames—the hayricks and wooden sheds about it causing the fire to run rapidly, fanned by a gentle breeze, which carried the smoke and sparks towards our lines. Sir de Lacy rode towards the left to get rid of this annoyance, and to rest his men, and as he did so, the round shot came bounding among the men lying down just before us. From the groans and stifled cries, it was too plain they left dead and dying in their course.

The Rifles in advance of our left were sharply engaged with the enemy in the vineyard, and, anxious to see what was going on, I rode over in that direction, and arrived at the place where were stationed the staff of the Light Division.

Sir George Brown looked full of fight, clean-shaven, neat and compact; I could not help thinking, however, there was a little pleasant malice in his salutation to me. As he rode past, he said in a very jaunty, Hyde Park manner, 'It's a very fine day, Mr Russell.'

At this moment the whole of our right was almost obscured by the clouds of black smoke from the burning village and the front of the Russian line above us had burst into a volcano of flame and white smoke—the roar of artillery became terrible—we could hear the heavy rush of the shot, those terrible dumps into the ground, and the crash of the trees, through which it tore with resistless fury and force; splinters and masses of stone flew out of the walls.

It was rather provoking to be told so coolly it was a very

fine day amid such circumstances; but at that very moment
the men near us were ordered to advance, and they did so
in quick time in open line towards the walls which bounded
the vineyards before us. ◉

It must certainly have been tempting to the leaders of the
army to mock poor Russell; to adopt a 'we told you so'
attitude, now that the fighting war had started. But if they
expected him to be frightened away from the place where
the action was, they were disappointed. Refusing to be
panicked he goes on . . .

◉ As I had no desire to lead my old friends of the Light
Division into action, I rode towards the right to rejoin Sir
de Lacy Evans, if possible; and as I got on to the road, I
saw Lord Raglan's staff riding towards the river, and the
shot came flinging close to me, one, indeed, killing one of the
bandsmen who were carrying a litter close to my side, after
passing over the head of my horse. It knocked away the
side of his face, and he fell dead—a horrible sight.

The batteries of the Second Division were unlimbered in
front, and were firing with great steadiness on the Russians;
and now and then a rocket, with a fiery tail and a huge
waving mane of white smoke, rushed with a shrill shout
against the enemy's massive batteries.

Before me all was smoke—our men were lying down still;
but the Rifles, led by Major Norcott, conspicuous on a black
horse, were driving back the enemy's sharp-shooters with
signal gallantry, and clearing the orchards and vineyards in
our front by a searching fire.

My position was becoming awkward. Far away in the
rear was the baggage, from which one could see nothing; but
where I was placed was very much exposed. A shell burst
over my head, and one of the fragments tore past my face
with an angry whir-r-r, and knocked up the earth at my
poor pony's feet.

Close at hand, and before me, was a tolerably good stone

house, one storey high, with a large court-yard, in which were several stacks of hay that had not as yet caught fire.

I rode into this yard, fastened up my pony to the rope binding one of the ricks, and entered the house, which was filled with fragments of furniture, torn paper, and books, and feathers, and cushion linings, and established myself at the window, from which I could see the Russian artillerymen serving their guns, their figures, now distinctly revealed against the hillside, and again lost in a spurting whirl of smoke.

I was thinking what a terrible sort of field-day this was, and combating an uneasy longing to get to the front, when a tremendous crash, as though a thunderclap had burst over my head, took place right above me, and in the same instant I was struck and covered with pieces of broken tiles, mortar and stones, the window out of which I was looking flew into pieces, parts of the roof fell down, and the room was filled with smoke.

There was no mistaking this warning to quit. A shell had burst in the ceiling. As I ran out into the yard I found my pony had broken loose, but I easily caught him and scarcely had I mounted when I heard a tremendous roll of musketry on my left front, and looking in that direction, I saw the lines of our red jackets in the stream, and swarming over the wooden bridge.

A mass of Russians were at the other side of the stream, firing down on them from the high banks, but the advance of the men across the bridge forced these battalions to retire; and I saw, with feelings which I cannot express, the Light Division, scrambling, rushing, foaming like a bloody surge up the ascent, and in a storm of fire, bright steel and whirling smoke, charge towards the deadly epaulement, from which came roar and flash incessantly.

I could distinctly see Sir George Brown and the several mounted officers above the heads of the men, and could detect the dark uniforms of the Rifles scattered here and there in front of the waving mass.

The rush of shot was appalling, and I recollect that I was particularly annoyed by the birds, which were flying about distractedly in the smoke, as I thought they were fragments of shell.

Already the wounded were passing by me. One man limped along with his foot dangling from the ankle, supporting himself on his firelock. 'Thank you kindly, sir,' he said, as I gave him a little brandy, the only drop I had left. 'Glory be to God, I killed and wounded some of the Russians before they crippled me, anyway.'

He halted off towards the rear. In another moment two officers approached—one leaning on the other—and both wounded, as I feared, severely. They went into the enclosure I had left, and having assured them I would bring them help, I rode off towards the rear and returned with the surgeon of the Cavalry Division, who examined their wounds.

All this time the roar of the battle was increasing. I went back to my old spot; in doing so I had to ride gently, for wounded men came along in all directions. One was cut in two by a round shot as he approached. Many of them lay down under the shelter of a wall, which was, however, enfiladed by the enemy.

Just at this moment I saw the Guards advancing in the most majestic and stately order up the hill, while through the intervals and at their flanks poured the broken masses of the Light Division, which their officers were busy in re-forming.

The Highlanders, who were beyond them, I could not see; but I never will forget the awful fury, the powerful detonation of the tremendous volleys which Guards and Highlanders* poured in upon the Russian battalions, which in vain

* Russell was mistaken; he was too remote to see that the Highlanders were too far to the right to be involved in this particular action

84

tried to defend their batteries and to check the onward march of that tide of victory . . .

The approach of the Light Division—why should I not dwell fondly on every act of that gallant body, the first 'put at' everything throughout the campaign?—was in double columns of brigades. Their course was marked by killed and wounded, for the Russians poured down a heavy vertical fire on our straggling lines.

They were straggling, but not weak; the whole Brigade, at a word from their officers, made a simultaneous rush up the bank and as they crowned it, met their enemies with a furious and close fire of their deadly rifles.

The dense battalions were smitten deeply and as the Light Division advanced to meet them, they rapidly fell back to the left, leaving many dead and wounded men close to the river's banks. ◉

More and more British soldiers plunged thigh deep into the river—running red now with the spilt blood of both armies. Maddened by thirst to the point where they became oblivious of flying shot and shell, many broke ranks to drink —or to pick grapes in the vineyards through which they passed.

But the advance did go on—and up—grimly, raggedly, with terrible losses but with enormous tenacity; until despite their favourable position, as the afternoon wore on the Russians were gradually forced back.

Finally the Brigade of Guards, still 'in perfect order' locked in hilltop combat with a (numerically) vastly superior division of Russian infantry.

As the gap between them closed, the Guards 'poured on their dense masses a fire so destructive that it annihilated the whole of their front ranks in an instant, and left a ridge of killed and wounded men on the ground'.

◉ The enemy, after a vain attempt to shake off the panic and disorder occasioned by that rain of death, renewed their fire very feebly for a few seconds, and then without waiting for a repetition of our reply, turned as our men advanced with bayonets at the charge, retreated over the brow of the hill, and marched off to join the mass of the Russian army, who were retreating with all possible speed . . .

It was near five o'clock. The Battle of the Alma was won. The men halted on the battlefield, and as the Commander-in-Chief, the Duke of Cambridge, Sir de Lacy Evans, and the other popular generals rode in front of the line, the soldiers shouted; and when Lord Raglan was in front of the Guards the whole army burst into a tremendous cheer which made one's heart leap.

The effect of that cheer can never be forgotten by those who heard it. ◉

September 1854. After the shouting and the triumph, came the long hours of tidying up.

◉ The Russian dead were all buried together in pits, and were carried down to their graves as they lay. Our parties buried 1,200 men. The British soldiers who fell were buried in pits in the same way. Their firelocks and the useful portions of their military equipment were alone preserved.

It was a sad sight to see the litters borne in from all quarters hour after hour—to watch the working parties as they wandered about the plain turning down the blankets which had been stretched over the wounded, to behold if they were yet alive, or were food for the worms, and then adding many a habitant to the yawning pits which lay with insatiable mouths gaping on the hillside—or covering up the poor sufferers destined to pass another night of indescribable agony.

The thirst of the wounded seemed intolerable, and our men—all honour to the noble fellows—went about relieving the wants of the miserable creatures as far as they could.

Scarlet poppies (*The Battle of the Alma*)

The quantity of firelocks, of greatcoats, of bearskin caps, of shakoes, of Russian helmets and flat forage caps, of knapsacks, of cross and sling belts, bayonets, cartouch-boxes, cartridges, swords, lying all over the hills, exceeded all computation; and round shot, fragments of shell smeared with blood and hair, grape-shot, Minié balls and bullets, were under the foot and eye at every step.

No ensign, eagle, standard or colour of any kind was displayed by the enemy, or found on the field. Our regiments marched with their colours, as a matter of course, and the enemy made the latter a special mark for the rifles. Thus it was so many ensigns, lieutenants and sergeants fell.

The sad duty of burying the dead was completed on the 22nd. The wounded were collected and sent on board ship in arabas and litters, and the surgeons with humane barbarity were employed night and day in saving life.

There was more than an acre of Russian wounded when they were brought and disposed on the ground. Our men were sent to the sea three miles distant on jolting arabas or tedious litters. The French had well-appointed covered hospital vans to hold ten or twelve men, drawn by mules, and their wounded were sent in much greater comfort than our poor fellows.

Not only the wounded but the sick were sent on board the fleet, the Russian officers who were wounded, and all prisoners of rank likewise. We have 1,000 sick on board, in addition to our wounded . . .

We might have expected—or rather if we had not known too well how unreasonable it would have been to expect much from such a source—we might have relied on more efficient assistance in our duty of burying the dead, and collecting and carrying the wounded on board, from the Admiral in command of the fleet.

Had a couple of thousand seamen and marines been landed, they could have done all that was required, have released us from two days' fearful duty, enabled us to follow the footsteps of our flying enemy, and to have completed his signal discomfiture, and have in all probability contributed materially to the issue of the campaign. ◉

But the army was still encamped on the heights above the Alma on September 22nd, and . . .

◉ Many men died of cholera in the night. My sleep was disturbed by the groans of the dying, and on getting up in the morning I found the corpse of a Russian outside the tent in which I had been permitted to rest. He was not there when we retired, so that the wretched creature, who had probably been wandering about without food upon the hills ever since the battle, must have crawled down towards our fires and there expired in the attempt to reach them: several men died in a similar way close to the tent. ◉

Late that night:

◉ . . . orders were sent round the divisions to be prepared for marching after daybreak, and early this morning [the 23rd] we left the bloodstained heights of the Alma—a name which will be ever memorable in history . . . ◉

It was too late. Had the allied armies followed up their incredible victory without delay, a great deal of pain and suffering might have been saved; but, as usual, immense mistakes were made, no forward reconnaissance was carried out to discover the state of the (as it happens, ill-repaired and under-manned) northern fortifications of Sebastopol; and so while the weary, but triumphant, British and French armies buried their dead and lugged the sick and wounded down to the sea-shore for embarkation to the already over-burdened, under-equipped, stinking and lousy hospital transports, the generals argued, and precious time and opportunity to finish off the war quickly were lost.

Had they not been, few people might have heard of William Howard Russell, and the good which came out of tragedy through the medium of his pen might have waited long years to reach fruition.

As it was, unaware of the weakness of the northern defences of Sebastopol, the generals decided on a long 'flanking' march to Balaklava, a small sea-port south of their objective.

7
Balaklava Bay is like a highland tarn

September 1854. Another dawn broke to what the gods in their omniscience must have found an ironic sound:

◉ . . . the French assembled all their drums and trumpets on the top of the highest of the hills they carried, and a wild flourish and roll, repeated again and again, and broken by peals of rejoicing from the bugles of the infantry, celebrated their victory ere they departed in search of the enemy. It was spirit-stirring and thrilling music and its effect as it swelled through the darkness of early morning down over the valley can never be forgotten.

Our watch-fires were still burning languidly as the sleepers roused themselves, all wet with dew, and prepared to leave the scene of their triumphs. The fogs of the night crept slowly up the hillsides and hung in uncertain folds round their summits, revealing here and there the gathering columns of our regiments in dark patches on the declivities, or showing the deep black-looking squares of the French battalions, already in motion towards the south.

Dimly seen in the distance, the fleet was moving along slowly by the line of the coast, the long plumes of smoke trailing back on their wake.

But what was that grey mass on the plain, which seemed settled down upon it almost without life or motion? Now and then, indeed, an arm might be seen waved aloft, or a man raised himself for a moment, looked around, and then fell down again.

Alas! That plain was covered with wounded Russians. Nearly sixty long hours they passed in agony upon the ground, and with but little hope of help or succour; we were compelled to leave them. Seven hundred and fifty wounded men, and we could do nothing for them. Their wounds had been bound and dressed, we had done all we could for them, and were obliged to depart . . .

In order to look after their wounds, an English surgeon was left behind with these seven hundred and fifty men. This most painful and desolate duty devolved on Dr Thomson, of the 44th regiment. He was told his mission would be his protection in case the Cossacks came, and that he was to hoist a flag of truce should the enemy appear in sight; and then, provided with some rum, biscuit and salt meat he was left alone with his charge, attended only by a single servant.

It was nearly eight o'clock ere the tents of headquarters were struck and the march began . . .

The country through which we marched was hilly and barren. Amidst steep hillocks covered with thistles, and separated from each other at times by small patches of steppe, wound the road to Sebastopol—a mere beaten track marked with cart-wheels, hoofs, and gun-carriage wheels.

We advanced uninterruptedly at an average rate of two and a quarter miles an hour, halting occasionally to rest the troops and allow the baggage waggons to come up.

At three o'clock the beautiful valley of the Katscha came in sight, its opposite side formed by a ridge of hills clad with verdure and small forests of shrubs, through which here and there shone the white walls of villas and snug cottages . . .

The first villa we came to was the residence of a physician or country surgeon. It had been ruthlessly destroyed by the Cossacks. A verandah laden with clematis, roses and honeysuckle in front was filled with broken music-stools, worktables and lounging chairs. All the glasses of the windows were smashed.

Everything around betokened the hasty flight of the inmates . . . The wine casks were broken and the contents spilt; the barley and corn of the granary were thrown about all over the ground; broken china and glass . . . were scattered over the pavement outside the kitchen—and amid all the desolation and ruin of the place, a cat sat blankly on the threshold winking her eyes in the sunshine at the newcomers. ◉

It was a scene familiar to victorious advancing battalions throughout history: the vicious, wanton destruction of a defeated army in retreat, working off its frustration. Russell's eagle eye missed not a single detail.

◉ . . . beds had been ripped open and the feathers littered the rooms a foot deep; chairs, sofas, fauteuils, bedsteads, book-cases, picture-frames, images of saints, women's needle-work, chests of drawers, shoes, boots, books, bottles, physic jars, all smashed or torn in pieces, lay in heaps. . . . Even the walls and doors were hacked with swords.

The physician's account-book lay open on a broken table: he had been stopped in the very act of debiting a dose to some neighbour, and his entry remained unfinished. Beside his account-book lay a volume of *Madame de Sévigné's Letters* in French, and a pharmacopœia in Russian.

A little bottle of prussic acid lay so invitingly near a box of bon-bons that I knew it would be irresistible to the first hungry private who had a taste for almonds, and I accordingly poured away the contents to prevent the possible catastrophe . . . ◉

The allies pushed on to the village of Eskel, on the banks

of the River Katscha, where they camped for the night. Every house and villa they came to was a scene of similar destruction. They found, however, one piano 'retained enough of its vital organs to breathe out *God Save the Queen* from its lacerated brass ribs, and it was made to do so accordingly—ay, under the very eyes of a rigid portrait of his Imperial Majesty the Czar which hung on the wall above!'

From the local inhabitants, who gradually crept out of hiding, they learned of the arrival of the Russians after the Battle of the Alma 'in a rather fatigued and dispirited condition'; of how, at this point, they had divided into two sections, one marching inland to the town of Bakschiserai and the rest southwards to Sebastopol, where they entered the city 'in some disorder'.

All along the road the allies were to find evidence of this hasty withdrawal: '. . . linstocks, cartridges, shakoes and caps . . . all the way'. In one house the allies occupied, 'books on strategy in Russian lay on the floor, and a pair of epaulettes, which seemed to have belonged to a Colonel, were found in a passage looking as if they had been torn from the shoulders . . .' A summary demotion, perhaps, of some unfortunate officer whose attempts to stem the allied advance had failed.

These warlike mementoes were not the only things left behind by the Russians. On the battlefield of the Alma itself evidence that the allies were not the only ones to bring an 'audience' to their fighting included a picnic basket, with six cold chickens and two bottles of champagne . . . a number of ladies' shawls and parasols, a lady's bonnet 'very nicely trimmed' and, most incredible of all—a petticoat!

A special viewing platform, it was later learned, had been erected so that the Russian ladies could watch the 'defeat of the invading armies' more easily, through their pearl-handled opera glasses.

One of the greatest examples ever of wishful war-reporting

occurred while the allies were making their way southwards. Although Russell rarely used it and always (as it now happened, with justification) distrusted it, the telegraph was actually in operation during the Crimean War and by its means brief 'news flashes' were sometimes sent ahead of the more detailed sea-borne dispatches. One such, sent shortly after the Battle of the Alma, was to the effect that this triumph had been followed, within days, by the storming and overthrow of the fortress of Sebastopol.

It was several days before a correction was made, and a fortnight before the slower methods which carried Russell's account of what happened reached London. The disappointment which followed the realisation that the war was still far from over was to add fuel to a fire of indignation already smouldering, and due very shortly to explode into flame.

Russell's own memories of the second half of the march south were by his own standards somewhat hazy. For the first time the hardships and hazards of his new profession brought him low.

◉ On the day of our march from the Katscha I was struck down by fever, fell from my pony into the stream where he was drinking, and was placed by one of the staff surgeons in a jolting araba carrying a part of the baggage of the Light Division. I saw but little that day except the march of men and the fine country around us . . . ◉

Fever or no, however, he kept his eyes open, and missed little of the sheer destructive power of men in large numbers, in victory as well as defeat.

◉ . . . the sun was exceedingly powerful and when from the top of a wooded hill we saw the delicious valley of the Belbeck studded with little snow-white cottages, with stately villas, with cosy snug-looking hamlets buried in trees, and fringed with a continuous line of the most gloriously green vineyards and the noblest orchards of fruit trees, there was an exclamation, a murmur of delight throughout the whole army, which precipitating itself like a torrent down the steep slopes of the hillsides, soon swarmed in every garden and clustered in destructive swarms around every bush.

Their halt was, however, a short one. The word was given to push over the stream, and its bright waters were soon defiled by the tramp of many feet.

Just as the araba in which I lay was passing a beautiful little chateau said to belong to a Russian general, I saw a stream of soldiers issue from it, laden with the most incongruous, but at the same time the richest, spoils which a man of taste and wealth could abandon to an enemy; others were engaged inside in smashing the house to atoms . . .

Shocked by such wanton outrage I inquired the cause and learned from an officer who was standing by that the soldiers had not done the smallest mischief till they saw an English staff officer of rank take a bronze statuette out of the house and ride away with it, whereupon the cry arose, 'Let us plunder too, if our officer sets the example.' ◉

After struggling up the steep, thickly wooded slope of the south side of the River Belbeck, camp was made on the southern ridge. Reinforcements were landed from the *Himalaya* and the French fleet.

It was a disturbed night. There were outbursts of firing from the Russians ('It is not pleasant,' Russell observed, 'to be roused up out of one's sleep by such violent noises at one o'clock in the morning . . .') and the spread of cholera among the troops continued.

At seven o'clock the Commanders held a conference, at which it was decided to press on to Balaklava along a high ridge.

Some of the party were actually within gunshot range of Sebastopol for part of the journey and Lord Raglan was startled, on emerging from a wooded road on to an open space, to encounter a body of Russian infantry—the baggage guard of a large detachment of the Russian army marching from Sebastopol to Bakschiserai. It is debatable which of the two parties was the more surprised.

⊙ They were not more than a few hundred yards distant. Lord Raglan simply turned his horse, and accelerating his pace, he and his staff quietly cantered back to the rear of the first division of Artillery.

The cavalry were quickly got in front—the guns were un-limbered and opened on the retreating mass of the Russians; the 2nd battalion of Rifles in skirmishing order threw in a volley of Minié balls, the cavalry executed a charge, and the result was that after a few rounds the Russians broke and fled along the road in great haste, leaving behind them an enormous quantity of baggage of every description for two miles strewed over the ground in the direction of their flight . . .

This was fair and legitimate plunder and the troops were halted and allowed to take what they liked. They broke open all the carts and tumbled out the contents on the road, but the pillage was conducted with regularity and the officers presided over it to see that there was no squabbling and that no man took more than his share.

Immense quantities of wearing apparel, of boots, shirts, coats, dressing cases, valuable ornaments and some jewellery were found in the baggage carts, as well as a military chest containing some money (there are people who say it held £3,000).

A Russian artillery officer was found in one of the carriages in a very jovial mood and had evidently been making rather free with the bottle. Plenty of champagne was discovered among the baggage and served to cheer the captors during their cold bivouac that night.

A great number of very handsome hussar jackets richly

laced with silver and made of fine light-blue cloth, which had never yet been worn, were also taken and sold by the soldiers for sums varying from 20*s* to 30*s* a piece. Fine large winter cloaks of cloth lined with rich furs were found in abundance.

The enemy were pursued two or three miles on the road to Bakschiserai, but they fled so precipitately the cavalry could not come up with them.

This plunder put the soldiers in great good humour, and they marched on the whole day in excellent spirits, leaving Sebastopol on their right . . .

Not the smallest attempt was made by the enemy to interrupt or annoy us during this very remarkable march, which could at any time have been greatly harassed by the least activity on the part of the Russians. Our march was through woods, along bad and often precipitous roads, and a few trees felled at intervals would have sufficed to stop the army for hours . . . ◉

Early the next morning the British and French armies crossed the last of the four rivers which punctuated their march, the Tchernaya, and were within a few miles of a place, the name of which was to ring down the years with the discordancy and foreboding of a fractured bell: Balaklava.

◉ I never was more astonished in my life than when on the morning of Tuesday, September 26th, I halted on the top of one of the numerous hills of which this portion of the Crimea is composed, and looking down saw under my feet a little pond, closely compressed by the sides of high rocky mountains; on it floated some six or seven English ships, for which exit seemed quite hopeless.

The bay is like a highland tarn, some half a mile in length from the sea, and varies from 250 to 120 yards in breadth. The shores are so steep and precipitous that they shut out as it were the expanse of the harbour, and make it appear

Allied ships crammed into the tiny harbour of Balaklava
(photographed by Roger Fenton, 1855)

much smaller than it really is. Towards the sea the cliffs close up and completely overlap the narrow channel which leads to the haven, so that it is quite invisible.

On the south-east of the poor village, which struggles for existence between the base of the rocky hills and the margin of the sea, are the extensive ruins of a Genoese fort, built some 200 feet above the level of the sea. It must have once been a large and important position, and its curtains, bastions, towers and walls, all destroyed and crumbling into decay though they are, evince the spirit and enterprise of the hardy seamen who penetrated these classic recesses so long ago. ◉

From almost every point except its proximity, Balaklava was totally unsuitable as a base from which to attack

Sebastopol. The harbour—that 'highland tarn'—was far too small to accommodate the British and French fleets, and the town itself, a Greek colony crowded between mountains and water, was little more than a fishing-village-cum-summer resort for Sebastopol.

Its pretty villas and flower-filled gardens were soon swarming with soldiers, trampling down the flowers, tearing down the vines and fruit trees, scattering their litter on land and in the water.

Lord Raglan entered the town about noon on September 26th. The cowed townsfolk:

⊙ . . . came out to meet him, bearing trays laden with fruit and flowers. Some of them bore loaves of bread cut up in pieces and placed on dishes covered with salt, in traditional token of good will and submission . . . ⊙

His Lordship assured them of his protection and then with a feeling of relief rode down to the beach to watch the British fleet steam in—or at least such of it as there was room for in the land-locked harbour. Now the army and navy were together again, and the army, at least, felt safer.

But the feeling of security was deceptive. The Russians may have been beaten at Alma and driven headlong towards Sebastopol and Bakschiserai, but dysentery and cholera were still stalking the allies. The sanitary facilities of Balaklava were quite inadequate to cope with an influx of 25,000 men— even fit ones. The town was soon in a revolting state and the stench which had accompanied the army for most of its miserable journey hung over it like a miasma. Lord Raglan ordered a cleaning-up operation, but there was no one to obey the order.

Very wisely, his Lordship removed himself from the town and established his headquarters in a 'snug farmhouse, surrounded by vineyards and extensive out-offices, about four and a half miles from Balaklava', from which he could see Sebastopol plainly.

The interior of an officer's hut at Balaklava

The poor soldiers were less lucky. Apart from the dirt and smells, medicines were in short supply. And the enemy 'amused themselves firing shot and shell over the heads of our artillery so that General Cathcart (Commander of the 4th Division) was obliged to move his quarters'.

Eventually the men themselves were moved into newly-landed tents, on the bleak heights above the little town. Food and water, at least, became more plentiful; but it was bitterly cold at night.

Still the allied Commanders could not agree on a plan for taking Sebastopol. The French favoured a siege. The British wanted to assault the city at once; but the southern fortifications proved stronger than expected and there was more dissension among the Generals—jealousy, childish bouts of sulking about rank and seniority.

As usual, in the end Lord Raglan bowed to the French decision and the two armies, the Russian in the great stronghold of Sebastopol and the allied in and around Bala-klava, settled down to wait.

Twenty-eight thousand Russians, confident in the impregnability of their fortress, which they were strengthening still further every day, were waiting for a move from the allies; the allies waited for the Russians to be starved out—a rather unlikely event since Sebastopol was still approachable from the sea, and from the north bank of the Tchernaya estuary.

Occasional and sometimes ludicrous skirmishes, in which neither side was prepared to attack before the other made a move, took place on the high plain between the two towns, but that was all. Obsessed with their own personal importance, the Generals continued to bicker among themselves.

8

Men must die

September/October 1854. While the troops settled in at Bala-klava, back in London the nation was still smarting over its disappointment about the fictitious report that Sebastopol had fallen. Russell's vivid and heart-rending dispatches describing the plight of the troops dying from cholera had been causing rumbles of anger for some time. These would have been louder had not Britain itself been in the grip of a similar epidemic. During 1854 no fewer than 10,000 people died of cholera in London alone, a fact which to a certain extent minimised the tragedy taking place in Bulgaria and Russia.

The trouble was that the root cause of cholera—a comparatively 'new' disease in Europe—was not at the time understood. Even eminent medical men of the day believed it was spread, not by water and insanitary conditions, but by 'poisonous vapours' which rose from the earth in certain places, at certain times. Russell himself had already written that 'the lake and the stream (near the camp at Aladyn) exhaled death, and at night fat unctuous vapours rose fold after fold from the valleys and crept up in the dark and stole into the tent of the sleeper and wrapped him in their deadly embrace . . .'

However, hard on the heels of Russell's ringing reports of victory on the heights above the Alma came follow-up dispatches from *The Times*'s resident correspondent in Constantinople, Thomas Chenery, who witnessed the arrival at Scutari of the hospital transports Russell had seen leaving the Crimea, half-sinking under their loads of human misery.

Chenery's indignation over the conditions which awaited the sick and injured men at Scutari was as great, and almost as graphic, as Russell's own. The only people available to help the wounded, he announced, were a group of Chelsea pensioners who had been sent out to Turkey as an ambulance corps.

⊙ Whether it was a scheme for saving money by utilizing the poor old men, or shortening the duration of their lives and pensions it is difficult to say [he reported acidly] but they have been found in practice rather to require nurses themselves than to be able to nurse others. . . . The man who conceived the idea that the hard work of a military hospital could be performed by worn-out and aged cripples must have had slight knowledge of warfare—or have profited little by experience . . . ⊙

He went on to describe the arrival of the hospital ships:

⊙ A few of the wounded were well enough to walk, and crept along, supported by a comrade, one with his arm in a sling, another with his trousers cut open from the hip to the knee and the thigh swathed in bandages, another with his hair clotted with blood and a ghastly wound on the face or head. On many the marks of approaching death were set . . .

All that the vigilant attendance of devoted officers can do is being done; for though only actively employed since the return of the first sick from the Crimea, many of the surgeons seem, through excess of work, almost as exhausted as those under their care . . . ☉

A day or so later a further burst of vituperation appeared in *The Times* from Chenery's pen. He had now had more time to look into the conditions under which the men had been brought from the battlefield to Scutari.

After beginning with praise for the crews of the British ships, who had struggled against desperate odds to keep their ships clean and fit for the men to travel in, and the hopelessly inadequate medical supervision aboard, he let fly about the general situation at the hospital to which the men had been so painfully transported:

☉ It is with feelings of surprise and anger that the public will learn that no sufficient preparations have been made for the cure of the wounded. Not only are there not sufficient surgeons . . . not only are there no dressers and nurses . . . but what will be said when it is known that there is not even linen to make bandages for the wounded . . .

Can it be said that the battle of the Alma has been an event to take the world by surprise? Has not the expedition to the Crimea been the talk of the last four months? And when the Turks gave up to our use the vast barracks to form a hospital and depot, was it not on the ground that the loss of the English troops was sure to be considerable? And yet after the troops have been six months in the country there is no preparation for the commonest surgical operations!

Not only are the men kept, in some cases, for a week without the hand of a medical man coming near their wounds —not only are they left to expire in agony, unheeded and shaken off, though catching desperately at the surgeon whenever he makes his rounds through the fetid ships, but now, when they are placed in the spacious building where we were led to believe that everything was ready which could ease their pain and facilitate their recovery, it is found that the commonest appliances of a workhouse sick ward are wanting and that the men must die through the medical staff of the British Army having forgotten that old rags are necessary for the dressing of wounds . . . ⊙

The next day he followed up with a second, equally angry and descriptive, report calling for more medical aid.

The Editor of *The Times* was not slow to see that this was all good, heady, journalistic material, and lost no time in backing up his team with a rousing Editorial on the same day.

He began by haranguing those readers 'sitting by their firesides devouring the morning paper in luxurious solitude, lazily tracing the path of conquest on one of Arrowsmith's best maps, counting the days of Sebastopol . . .' and regarding the war as an 'amusing spectacle', while other 'poor fellows are going through innumerable hardships, to bite the

The hospital in Sebastopol; this is typical of the hospitals of both sides

dust at last in mortal agony before a Russian redoubt'.

◉ But [thundered Delane] while we are all in the third heaven of martial ecstasy, there is one little consideration that must now and then abate the sublimity of our enjoyment. What are we doing for the cause we have so much at heart? . . . Soldiers and sailors are not the savage, murderous, ravaging and destroying creatures they are sometimes imagined . . . Till they are dying of hunger and thirst, or have seen their comrades falling all round them, they are the merest sheep . . . The wolves are those who stay at home, blow up the angry passions of the war, and feed its perpetual resentments . . . ◉

After a great deal more in similar vein, *The Times*'s Editor called for action, and, even more important, money, to help right the mistakes of omission which had led to the appalling situation in Turkey. Four or five thousand pounds, Delane modestly suggested, would do a great deal to help.

In the event he received much more than that. Throughout the autumn and winter of 1854/55 more than £20,000 was collected for *The Times*'s Fund and depots were set up all over the country for the collection of clean linen, to be made into bandages and dressings.

Many readers wrote to *The Times* making suggestions for raising money. (The whole of the staff of the Crystal Palace donated a day's pay, and the lessee of the Victoria Theatre offered the receipts of one night's performance.)

One reader, who signed her letter 'A sufferer by the Present War', described the agony of wives and mothers wondering whether, during a man's last moments, 'was there no one near to relieve his sufferings, to speak a word of kindness or hope, to receive some last message, perhaps for some dear ones at home, or even to support his head or give him a drink of water . . .'

She went on to suggest that it was, in fact, women rather than men who were needed to help the wounded and sick.

'There are,' she pointed out, 'numbers of able-bodied and tender-hearted Englishwomen who would joyfully and with alacrity go out to devote themselves to nursing the sick and wounded, if they could be associated for that purpose and placed under proper protection . . . Women are, after all, the best nurses. They are in their element in a hospital, moving quickly and quietly here and there administering not physical aid alone . . .'

There was indeed in England at that moment one such woman who was not only ready and willing, but who had been waiting and preparing herself for this opportunity for many years. Her name was Florence Nightingale. After only a feeble attempt to persuade the country that all was really well in the hospitals in Turkey, the Government accepted her offer of help.

By October 21st Miss Nightingale had recruited her first staff of thirty-eight—not without some difficulty in spite of *The Times*'s lady-correspondent's confident predictions. In the end the party consisted of fourteen hospital nurses and twenty-four nuns and Anglican sisters: a motley crew. But they were better than nothing, and Miss Nightingale was a formidable organiser. They set out, with the approval, help, and full backing of the War Office, for Scutari—and the rest is not only history, but legend.

Russell himself saw very little at firsthand of Florence Nightingale's work. Being continuously in the front line he saw, and wrote of, only the horrific conditions which existed there. Florence Nightingale rarely moved from Scutari, on the far side of the Black Sea, where her hands were more than full battling with the overwhelming problems of running a hospital against defeating odds. During one month-long period she spent in the Crimea, Russell himself was for much of the time absent on an expedition elsewhere.

Remarkable as she was, the men in the Crimea really needed a dozen Florence Nightingales in Scutari. Unfortunately such people do not come in dozens. The miracle was that even one of them existed at such a time.

And while the Black Sea was dotted with slowly-creeping ships, each one 'a mess of putridity' on which 'neglected gunshot wounds bred maggots which crawled in every direction, infecting the food . . .' Lord Cardigan's yacht, complete with French chef, sailed into Balaklava harbour. From then on, when not actually fighting, the noble lord commanded the Light Brigade from its plushy comfort—and a distance of several miles.

9
No drums, no bugle-calls

October 1854. Winter was drawing on. The atmosphere in the British camp was sombre. Russell wrote:

⊙ No drums, no bugle-calls, no music of any kind, was ever heard within our precincts, while our neighbours (the French) close by kept up incessant rolls, fanfaronnades and flourishes, relieved every evening by the fine performances of their military bands.

The fact was many of our instruments had been placed in store and the regimental bands were broken up and disorganised, the men being devoted to the performance of the duties for which the ambulance corps was formed.

I think, judging from one's own feelings, and from the expressions of those around, that the want of music in camp was productive of graver consequences than appeared likely to occur at first blush from such a cause. Every military man knows how regiments, when fatigued on the march, cheer up at the strains of their band, and dress up, keep step and walk on with animation and vigour when it is playing . . . ◉

In short, apart from their military ineptitude, the generals seemed ignorant of one of the most important aspects of warfare—the need to keep up morale—which can never have been more necessary in any war than it was in the Crimea.

Gradually the inactivity began to get on everyone's nerves. The sense of euphoria following the victory at Alma, and the Russians' undignified retreat, faded. Trench-digging in the stony earth was hard going. It was the more maddening that the Russians could be seen, quite clearly, strengthening their own defences.

These defences, facing south-east where the allies were encamped, formed an irregular convex curve, with fortified points jutting out at intervals, the total length being about five miles. One of the strong points, in a central position, was known as The Redan; the one next to it The Malakoff. Both these fortifications were to be of immense importance to the allies, whose own front stretched for seven or eight miles in a concave curve roughly following the lines of the city walls, and consisting mainly of trenches dug under cover of darkness, and sometimes under fire from the Russian guns.

From a mile and a half away, Russell watched the Russians at work inside their fortress.

◉ I am now sitting on the wall of a ruined farmhouse, which serves as a picquet post for the Third Division, and from which I can look down on the town of Sebastopol. It shines, white and clear, in the fine October sun, and, on a first view, it seems open and defenceless on the south and south-east side.

The Russians are plainly visible through the glass, working like bees; women and children are carrying up earth in baskets, and already the white tower on the right of our lines is blocked up with a double line of earthworks pierced for guns.

The fort is no longer the white fort—it has been painted a buff colour, probably not to look so conspicuous at night. . . . Large masses of men are . . . at drill on parade on a piece of land inside the camp . . . There are a few Cossacks prowling about in front . . . watching our motions . . .

There is nothing doing in our front, but in the rear the sailors are busy dragging up guns and carriages . . . ☉

At last, on October 17th, a bombardment was opened up on the defences of Sebastopol. Orders were given to concentrate as far as possible on the Russian military installations, and to spare the town itself. All day long on the 17th and 18th the guns thundered out on both sides. Russell gave a remarkable running commentary on the progress of the engagement. At 8.40 a.m. on October 17th, he reported:

☉ . . . the French magazine in the extreme right battery of twelve guns blew up with a tremendous explosion, killing and wounding 100 men. The Russians cheered, fired with renewed vigour, and crushed the French fire completely, so that they were not able to fire more than a gun now and then at intervals, and at ten o'clock they were nearly silenced on that side. ☉

Bombardment took place from the sea, as well as land.

☉ At 12.45 the French line-of-battle ships ran up in most magnificent style and engaged the batteries on the sea side. The scene was indescribable, and the Russians replying vigorously to the attacks by sea and land, though suffering greatly . . .

At 1.25 another magazine in the French batteries blew up. . . . The cannonade was tremendous. Our guns demolished the Round Tower, but could not silence the works around it . . .

At 1.40 a great explosion took place in the centre of Sebastopol amid much cheering from our men, but the fire was not abated. . . . At 2.25 a terrific explosion of a powder magazine took place in the Russian Redan Fort. The Russians, however, returned to their guns and still fired from the re-entering angle of their works. The cannonade was continuous from the ships and from our batteries, but the smoke did not permit us to see if the British fleet was engaged . . .

At 3.30 a loose powder store inside our naval battery was blown up by a Russian shell, but did no damage. The enemy's earth-works were much injured by our fire . . .

At 3.35 the magazine inside the works of the Round Fort was blown up by our shot.

At four the ships outside were ripping up the forts and stoneworks and town by tremendous broadsides. Only the French flag was visible, the English fleet being on the opposite side of the harbour . . .

. . . Towards dusk the fire slackened greatly, and at night it ceased altogether, the Russians for the first time being silent. The French have lost about 200 men, principally by the explosions; our loss is very small—under 100 killed and wounded since the siege began. ⊙

At times the fighting became less remote—sometimes almost farcical. A group of British riflemen, out on a skirmish, were surprised by a group of Russians in a quarry . . .

⊙ Our men had exhausted all their ammunition; but as soon as they saw the Russians they seized the blocks of stone which were lying about, and opened a vigorous volley on the enemy. The latter either had empty pouches or were so much surprised that they forgot to load, for they resorted to the same missiles. A short fight ensued, which ended in our favour, and the Russians retreated, pelted vigorously as long as the men could pursue them. ⊙

All told the pounding of Sebastopol lasted for nearly a week. Day after day the guns bellowed and grumbled. Smoke hung in a thick, acrid pall over the countryside. The smell of death and putrifaction, never far away in the Crimea, was heavy in the air. On October 22nd Russell reported:

⊙ A Pole and some Russians deserted last night. They

tell us that the enemy have lost 3,000 killed and wounded, that the town is in a frightful state—the shops closed, the merchants fled, the goods placed underneath in the cellars and that the 'pointed' balls and shells (Lancasters) do a frightful mischief.

There are no longer *volunteers* to work the guns, as there were at first. The men have now to be forced to the batteries. Many poor women and children have lost their lives in this terrible cannonade . . . ◉

In view of this information it seems incredible that the allies did not attack the town in a determined fashion and finish off the war, particularly as throughout the period of the bombardment the Russians continued to bring up reinforcements which they established in a village a few miles to the east; but once again the French refused to make a move, and Lord Raglan would not act on his own.

It is true that the allied forces were still in a very weak condition. The Russian guns may have killed comparatively few, but the shocking fact was that the British army had been slashed almost in half by sickness. On October 24th:

◉ About 500 men came today, as fit for service, from Scutari. They were landed at Balaklava, and proceeded to march out to their camps, but I regret to say that before they had marched many miles—indeed, there are not many to march—more of the poor fellows than it was pleasant to count fell out exhausted, proving that they had not quite recovered from their illness.

The diminution of our numbers every day is enough to cause serious anxiety. Out of 35,600 men borne on the strength of the army there are not more now than 16,500 rank and file fit for service. Since the 10th of this month upwards of 700 men have been sent as invalids to Balaklava. There is a steady drain of some forty or fifty men a day going out from us, which is not dried up by the numbers of the returned invalids. Even the twenty or thirty a day wounded and disabled, when multiplied by the number of days we have been here, becomes a serious item in the aggregate . . .

The Russian Governor sent in yesterday to Lord Raglan to ask for a days' truce to bury the dead on both sides. The same authority has it that Lord Raglan replied, 'he had no dead to bury'. The Russians, in revenge for this, are leaving their dead where they fall outside the lines, and also bring them out from the town, and place them in the valley frequented by our picquets and skirmishers, who are much annoyed by the stench. This is a new engine of warfare . . . ◉

By the 24th October a Russian force of 25,000 men had been assembled—infantry, cavalry and guns. The next morning news came that this vast army was marching on Balaklava. At the end of that day Russell wrote one of the bloodiest, one of the most famous, one of the most shameful —and in some ways one of the bravest—pages in British history.

10
In all the pride and splendour of war
(The Battle of Balaklava)

October 25th, 1854. News came at dawn on October 25th of the Russian 'surprise' advance towards Balaklava. In spite of persistent rumours over the previous few days that this attack was imminent, the allied forces were not ready.

◉ Lord Lucan's little camp was the scene of great excitement. The men had not had time to water their horses;

they had not broken their fast from the evening of the day before, and had barely saddled at the first blast of the trumpet, when they were drawn up on the slope behind the redoubts in front of their camp, to operate on the enemy's squadrons. ⊙

It was eight o'clock before Lord Raglan and his staff turned out and 'cantered towards the rear of our position'.

Russell himself rode in the direction of the firing 'over the thistles and large stones which cover the undulating plain that stretches away towards Balaklava'. He was soon busy noting the disposition of the troops and—as always, with appreciation—the landscape and the weather.

⊙ Faint white clouds rose here and there over the hill from the cannonade below. Never did the painter's eye rest on a more beautiful scene than I beheld from the ridge. The fleecy vapours still hung around the mountain tops, and mingled with the ascending volumes of smoke; the patch of sea sparkled freshly in the rays of the morning sun, but its light was eclipsed by the flashes which gleamed from the masses of armed men below. ⊙

Russians were pouring over the mountain passes close to the River Tchernaya, to the south-east of Sebastopol; streaming into the valley leading down to Balaklava and the road up which supplies were brought to the encampments from the allied base. This road ran over a chain of hills—'Causeway Heights'—and was defended at this vulnerable point by a few Turkish-manned 'redoubts' (earthworks) and a handful of naval guns in the charge of British non-commissioned officers.

'Standing-to' on the plain below, overlooking Balaklava harbour, were the 93rd Highlanders, soon to become famous as Russell's 'thin red streak'.

The redoubts fell like nine-pins before the Russian advance, the Turks flying in panic.

⊙ They ran in scattered groups . . . towards Balaklava,

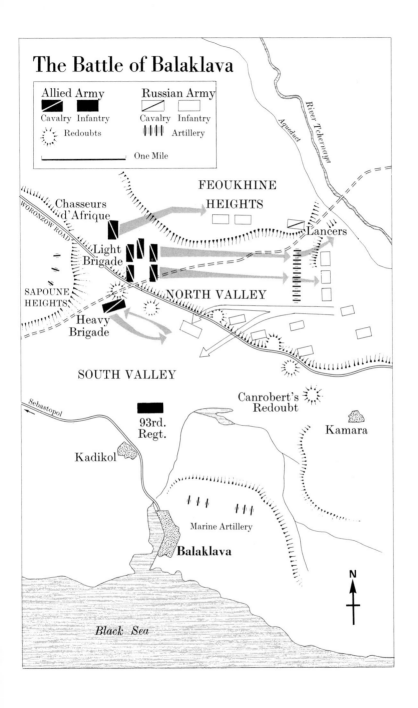

but the horse-hoof of the Cossack was too quick for them, and sword and lance were busily plied among the retreating herd. The yells of the pursuers and pursued were plainly audible [Russell wrote in some disgust]. ⊙

The allied naval guns were too far away to inflict any damage and the Turks in batteries along the French entrenchments too demoralised to fire accurately. The Russians swept on, exhilarated by their early, easy success.

At last, confronted by the unwavering Highlanders, they paused to consolidate . . .

⊙ . . . The Russian cavalry on the left . . . halt, and squadron after squadron flies up from the rear, till they have a body of some 1,500 men along the ridge—Lancers, and Dragoons, and Hussars. Then they move in two bodies, with another in reserve.

The cavalry who have been pursuing the Turks on the right are coming up to the ridge beneath us, which conceals our cavalry from them. The Heavy Brigade in advance is drawn up in two lines. . . . The Light Brigade is on their left, in two lines also.

The silence is oppressive; between the cannon bursts one can hear the champing of bits and the clink of sabres in the valley below.

The Russians on their left draw breath for a moment, and then in one grand line dash at the Highlanders. The ground flies beneath their horses' feet; gathering speed at every stride, they dash on towards that thin red streak topped with a line of steel.

The Turks fire a volley at eight hundred yards, and run. As the Russians come within six hundred yards, down goes that line of steel in front, and out rings a rolling volley of musketry. The distance is too great; the Russians are not checked . . .

With breathless suspense everyone awaits the bursting of the wave upon the line of Gaelic rock; but ere they come within a hundred and fifty yards, another deadly volley flashes from the levelled rifles, and carries death and terror into the Russians. They wheel about, open files right and left, and fly back faster than they came.

'Brave Highlanders! Well done!' shout the excited spectators. ◉

But the battle was far from over. It was the turn next of the cavalry—six hundred of the 'Heavy Brigade' under General Scarlett; the Greys and Enniskilleners—to meet the main body of the Russian cavalry, advancing on their left at an easy gallop over the ridge of Causeway Heights.

It was a brave stand against heavy odds; the Russian front line was 'at least double the length of ours . . . three times as deep' and behind it was another, equally strong and compact. The Scots and Irish horsemen were not intimidated by the superior numbers, though. The Russians advanced downhill to meet them at a slow canter, then at a trot. They had slowed almost to a halt, within a few hundred yards of

The Charge of the Heavy Brigade at Balaklava

the 'Heavies' when the trumpets rang out, and . . .

⊙ As lightning flashes through a cloud, the Greys and Enniskilleners pierced through the dark masses of Russians with a cheer that thrilled to every heart.

The shock was but for a moment. There was a clash of steel and a light play of sword blades in the air, and then the Greys and the red-coats disappear in the midst of the shaken, quivering columns.

In another moment we see them emerging and dashing on with diminished numbers, and in broken order, against the second line, which is advancing against them as fast as it can to retrieve the fortune of the charge.

It was a terrible moment. 'God help them! They are lost!' was the exclamation of more than one man, and the thought of many . . .

[But] . . . By sheer steel and sheer courage, Enniskillener and Scot were winning their desperate way right through the enemy's squadrons and already grey horses and red coats had appeared right at the rear of the second mass, when, with irresistible force, like one bolt from a bow the 1st Royals, the 4th Dragoon Guards, and the 5th Dragoon Guards rushed at the remnants of the first line of the enemy, went through it as though it were made of pasteboard, and, dashing on the second body of Russians as they were still disordered by the terrible assault of the Greys and their companions, put them to utter rout . . .

A cheer burst from every lip . . . officers and men took off their caps and shouted with delight . . . ⊙

The Russians retired in confusion, 'leaving the ground covered with horses and men'. The allies re-grouped, drew breath and strove to curb their jubilation, while the Commanding Officers reviewed the situation.

A vast question-mark hangs over the fifteen minutes which followed. Nobody, then or later, ever satisfactorily explained the curious events leading up to 'the melancholy catastrophe' which filled the watchers on the battlefield with consternation and for more than a century following inspired poets, tortured historians, caused rancour, bitterness, confusion and sorrow—and immortalised the names of those most closely concerned in what came to be known simply as The Charge of the Light Brigade.

It began, as so often, with muddle and misunderstanding. Lord Cardigan claimed that his hated rival (and superior officer) Lord Lucan had ordered him to remain in, and defend, a position five hundred yards from the Russian flank. To leave this, he declared, would have been to disobey clear-cut orders.

Lord Lucan's version was, of course, quite different and the argument as to who said, or meant, what, rumbled on for years after the war was over. But at the time Lord Cardigan, stubborn and glowering, and his cavaliers, fuming, sat and waited and watched—first the gallant actions of the 'Heavies' and then the headlong retreat of the Russians; and they did nothing (to everyone's astonishment) to turn that retreat into a rout.

Meanwhile Lord Raglan—remote on a hilltop from which he watched the action 'as though looking on the stage from the box of a theatre'—sent a series of little notes of instruction down to the fighting men on the 'stage' below. Some arrived too late to be of use, having been overtaken by events; but it was the fourth, to the Light Brigade, which set in train the really tragic events of the day.

It was carried, at his own request, by Captain Nolan of the 15th Hussars. Of him Russell wrote:

⊙ A braver soldier than Captain Nolan the army did not possess. He was known to all his arm of the service for his entire devotion to his profession. A matchless horseman and a first-rate swordsman his name must be familiar to all who take interest in our cavalry for his excellent work, published

117

a year ago, on our drill and system of remount and breaking horses.

I had the pleasure of his acquaintance and I know he entertained the most exalted opinions respecting the capabilities of the English horse soldier. Properly led [they] could in his mind break square, take batteries, ride over columns of infantry and pierce any other cavalry in the world as if they were made of straw.

He thought they had not had the opportunity of doing all that was in their power, and that they had missed even such chances as they had offered them—that in fact they were in some measure disgraced.

He rode off with his orders to Lord Lucan. He is now dead and gone. God forbid I should cast a shade on the brightness of his honour, but I am bound to state what I am told occurred when he reached his Lordship. ⊙

Before he did this, Russell detailed—by way of explaining the odds against which the British were pitched—the new layout of the battlefield.

⊙ . . . As the Russian cavalry retired, their infantry fell back towards the head of the valley, leaving men in three of the redoubts they had taken, and abandoning the fourth.

They had also placed some guns on the heights over their position on the left of the gorge. Their cavalry joined the reserves, and drew up in six solid divisions, in an oblique line, across the entrance to the gorge.

Six battalions of infantry were placed behind them, and about thirty guns were drawn up along their line, while masses of infantry were also collected on the hills behind the redoubts on our right.

Our cavalry had moved up to the ridge across the valley, on our left, as the ground was broken in front, and had halted . . .

When Lord Lucan received the order from Captain Nolan, and had read it, he asked, we are told, 'Where are we to advance to?'

Captain Nolan pointed with his finger to the line of the
Russians, and said: 'There are the enemy, and there are the
guns, sir, before them; it is your duty to take them,' or
words to that effect. ◉

The actual wording of the order runs as follows:

◉ Lord Raglan wishes the cavalry to advance rapidly to
the front—follow the enemy and try to prevent the enemy
carrying away the guns ... ◉

It is true that the wording of the note is vague, but since
the Russians were, at that moment, busy removing the
British naval guns from the redoubts they had overwhelmed
earlier, it now seems almost certain that Lord Raglan intended the attack to be made on them (captured guns being
a proof of victory in battle, and their removal to be prevented at almost any cost), *not* on the solid phalanx of Russian
troops now formed up in the valley, on which Russian
artillery was trained, and to which Captain Nolan pointed.

◉ It is a maxim of war [Russell wrote] that cavalry never
act without a support; that infantry should be close at hand
when cavalry carry guns, as the effect is only instantaneous,
and it is necessary to have on the flank of a line of cavalry
some squadrons in column, the attack on the flank being
most dangerous.

The only support our light cavalry had was the reserve of
heavy cavalry at a great distance behind them, the infantry
and guns being far in the rear.

There were no squadrons in column at all, and there was a
plain to charge over, before the enemy's guns were reached,
of a mile and a half in length. ◉

It seemed that Captain Nolan, anxious that the Light
Cavalry should be given their taste of glory at last, chose to
read Lord Raglan's message differently.

From the heights where the generals were gathered he
plunged down a narrow stony track to the valley entrance,

where the Light Brigade uneasily awaited their orders, the flimsy scrap of paper clutched in his hand.

And: '. . . there are the enemy . . . there are the guns . . . it is your duty to take them,' he ordered, pointing dramatically at the ranks of waiting Russians blocking the gorge.

◉ Lord Lucan, with reluctance, gave the order to Lord Cardigan to advance upon the guns, conceiving that his orders compelled him to do so. The noble Earl, though he did not shrink, also saw the fearful odds against him. Don Quixote in his tilt against the windmill was not so reckless as the gallant fellows who prepared without a thought to rush on almost certain death . . . ◉

It was one of the craziest moves in a war not notable for intelligent decisions. The whole brigade, Russell tells us, scarcely made one effective regiment, but even this could ill be spared. The 'noble Earl' did not of course argue or object —apart from his duty to carry out his orders, he was still not 'speaking' to his brother-in-law.

It was ten minutes past eleven when they moved off. As they did so Lord Cardigan was heard to murmur, 'Well, here goes the last of the Brudenells' (his family name).

Afterwards Russell tried, as best as one man could, to describe just what happened:

◉ As they rushed towards the front, the Russians opened on them from the guns in the redoubt on the right, with volleys of musketry and rifles. They swept proudly past, glittering in the morning sun in all the pride and splendour of war. We could scarcely believe the evidence of our senses. Surely that handful of men are not going to charge an enemy in position?

Alas! It was but too true—their desperate valour knew no bounds, and far indeed was it removed from its so-called better part—discretion.

They advanced in two lines, quickening their pace as they

closed towards the enemy. A more fearful spectacle was never witnessed than by those who, without the power to aid, beheld their heroic countrymen rushing to the arms of death.

At the distance of 1,200 yards the whole line of the enemy belched forth, from thirty iron mouths, a flood of smoke and flame, through which hissed the deadly balls. Their flight was marked by instant gaps in our ranks, by dead men and horses, by steeds flying wounded or riderless across the plain.

The first line is broken; it is joined by the second, they never halt or check their speed an instant; with diminished ranks, thinned by those thirty guns, which the Russian has laid with the most deadly accuracy, with a halo of flashing steel above their heads, and with a cheer which was many a noble fellow's death-cry, they flew into the smoke of the batteries, but ere they were lost to view the plain was strewed with their bodies and with the carcasses of horses.

They were exposed to an oblique fire of musketry. Through the clouds of smoke we could see their sabres flashing as they rode up to the guns and dashed between them, cutting down the gunners as they stood.

We saw them riding through the guns . . . to our delight

The Charge of the Light Brigade at Balaklava

we saw them returning, after breaking through a column of Russian infantry, and scattering them like chaff, when the flank fire of the battery on the hill swept them down, scattered and broken as they were.

Wounded men and dismounted troops flying towards us told the sad tale—demi-gods could not have done what they had tried to do.

At the very moment when they were about to retreat an enormous mass of Lancers was hurled at their flank. Colonel Shewell of the 8th Hussars saw the danger, and rode his few men straight at them, cutting his way through with fearful loss. The other regiments turned and engaged in a desperate encounter.

With courage too great almost for credence, they were breaking their way through the columns which enveloped them, when there took place an act of atrocity without parallel in the modern warfare of civilized nations.

The Russian gunners, when the storm of cavalry passed, returned to their guns. They saw their own cavalry mingled with the troopers who had just ridden over them, and to the eternal disgrace of the Russian name, the miscreants poured a murderous volley of grape and canister on the mass of struggling men and horses, mingling friend and foe in one common ruin.

It was as much as our Heavy Cavalry Brigade could do to cover the retreat of the miserable remnants of that band of heroes as they returned to the place they had so lately quitted in all the pride of life. At thirty-five minutes past eleven not a British soldier, except the dead and dying, was left in front of these bloody Muscovite guns.

Captain Nolan was killed by the first shot fired, as he rode in advance of the Hussars, cheering them on. Lord Lucan was slightly wounded. Lord Cardigan received a lance-thrust through his clothes . . .

While our affair was going on, the French cavalry made a

most brilliant charge at the battery on our left; but they could not get off the guns without support . . . The Heavy Cavalry moved slowly backwards, covering the retreat of the broken men.

The ground was left covered with our men and hundreds of the Russians . . . ◉

The whole action had taken less than half an hour. For the rest of the morning the fighting swayed backwards and forwards—a little ground was won, a little lost; the Russians were gradually pushed back into a position of near-impregnability and the allies' position became 'too large to be readily defended'. The allied generals then decided to content themselves with keeping Balaklava and the communications with it open by the westerly and southerly heights behind the camp.

◉ Lord Raglan continued on the hillside all day, watching the enemy. It was dark ere he returned to his quarters. With the last gleam of day we could see the sheen of the enemy's lances in their old position in the valley; and their infantry gradually crowned the heights on their left, and occupied the road to the village which is beyond Balaklava to the southward.

Our Guards were moving back as I passed them, and the tired troops were being replaced by a strong French division, which was marched down to the valley at five o'clock.

On the night of the 25th, when our guns were taken into Sebastopol, there was joy throughout the city, and it was announced that the Russians had gained a great victory. A salvo of artillery was fired, and at nine o' clock p.m. a tremendous cannonade was opened against all our lines by the enemy. It did no injury . . . ◉

The injury had all been done much earlier. Out of the 'gallant six hundred' 387 officers and men were dead, wounded or missing. A total of 520 horses was lost. The Russian 'victory' was far smaller than they claimed (they had not, after all, reached Balaklava) but for the allies nothing had been won—and they had lost control of the Woronzow road, the only road connecting Balaklava with their encampments on the heights before Sebastopol. In future they would have no direct lines of communication except rough mountain tracks, up which all equipment, food and ammunition would have to be carried.

11
Dreadful deeds of daring (The Battle of Inkerman)

October/November 1854. Long after the Crimean War was over, when Russell was reporting another great conflict, the Crown Prince of Prussia was to tell him: 'You are the hardest worker among us, for when our work is over and we can go to sleep, you have to begin and describe what has been done!'

What made it all the harder was that this work—which had to be done while his head was still full of sound and fury, his eyes blurred by smoke and sun-glare—was of the utmost delicacy and importance. Mistakes or distortions would be magnified out of all proportion when they appeared in print, to be scrutinised and analysed by experts and laymen alike.

He wrote under the greatest physical difficulties. Sometimes he had not eaten for many hours. After dark his only light was a candle thrust into the neck of a wine-bottle. (Sometimes he wrote so long that the candle 'disappeared in the bottle like a stage demon through a trap-door'.) Paper was often scarce, and he was occasionally reduced to manufacturing his own ink out of gunpowder.

Russell writing a dispatch in his tent during the winter of
1854–55

It is true he had the help of a servant—of sorts—who
collected his rations (grudgingly allotted to him by the
army) and generally ministered to his material needs, but
material needs were a comparatively minor problem. Towards
the end of October 1854 he tried, in one of his dispatches, to
give an honest picture of his greatest worry:

⊚ Not even the general who directs the operations can
describe a battle. It is proverbially impossible to do so. Who
can hope to satisfy every officer engaged when each colonel
in the smoke and tumult and excitement of the conflict sees
only what is done by his own men, and scarcely knows even
where the next regiment is? He beholds but the enemy before
him and that small portion of his regiment which may be
close to him at the time.

On looking at my own account of the battle of the Alma,
which was written literally on the field—part of it while
exposed to a broiling sun, the morning after the action, on
the grass, in the open air (for tents were rare coverings then,

125

and all that were on the heights were crowded); part while exposed to an incessant fire of small-talk in a tent full of excited and garrulous officers, I find I have made mistakes which I confess without a blush, and which I trust are excusable under the circumstances in which I was placed, especially when it was considered that the undertaking, under the most favourable conditions, is not an easy one. ⊙

Although he had a bird's eye view of the events of October 25th, and seems as sure of his facts as ever he was, other men's reports suggest that even at the Battle of Balaklava Russell was not infallible—that, for example, he exaggerated the exploits of the Highlanders, whose engagement, though important, was a comparatively minor one. Some even said they were never engaged by the Russians at all . . . it was simply their 'resolute bearing' which kept the enemy at bay.

But who is to say, more than a century later, which report was literally correct; or whose eyes were dazzled by the sun? And does it really matter? The important fact is that Russell's new-style, hard-hitting and brilliantly graphic dispatches opened the eyes not just of a nation, but virtually the whole civilised world to the realities, and the nastiness, of war; and set a pattern for war-reporting which still influences the correspondents of today.

It was only a matter of days after describing his difficulties that he was faced with one of the most confusing and perplexing war-reporting jobs of his career.

Slowly and carefully, almost painfully, over the years historians have collected and reconstructed individual incidents from the Battle of Inkerman and built them into a composite picture. It has taken time, and patience, and a period of tranquillity in which to view the happenings of November 5th, 1854, to achieve this. As for Russell . . .

⊙ No-one [he wrote when it was over] however placed, could have witnessed even a small portion of the doings of this eventful day, for the vapours, fog and drizzling mist obscured the ground where the struggle took place to such an extent as to render it impossible to see what was going on at the distance of a few yards.

'Besides this, the irregular nature of the ground, the rapid fall of the hill towards Inkerman, where the deadliest fight took place, would have prevented one under the most favourable circumstances seeing more than a very insignificant and detailed piece of the terrible work below. ◉

It all started confusingly, and with no warning. Russell had spent the previous evening convivially and, for the time, peacefully, with friends.

◉ My staff friend Stopford, Eber [another *Times* correspondent, with the Turkish troops] and I feasted on our rations, to which I added a tin of curried rabbit and some cheese; drank our tots of rum [and] smoked our pipes . . .

Before I retired for the night I went across to the lines where the horses stood under the shelter of an old wall, saw that some fodder I had brought up had been equally divided, and then turned in—i.e. kicked off riding-boots and got in between the tarpaulin coverlet and the rug, which was spread over a layer of straw—listened for a while to the drip of the rain, the thudding of the firing in the trenches, the stamping of the horses near at hand—and so to sleep, and to dream. ◉

The dreams were roughly interrupted. At five o'clock in the morning a rattle of musketry fire from the Inkerman ridge, just east of Sebastopol, jerked Russell into wakefulness.

He pulled on his boots, stuffed a lump of cheese, a few biscuits and a flask of rum into his pockets, lumbered across to his horse and heaved himself into the saddle.

In the grey pre-dawn swirling mist and drizzle it was difficult to see what was happening. A few pathetic little fires, a sign that the soldiers were preparing to cook breakfast, blinked here and there; candles gleamed in the windows of Lord Raglan's house, and lanterns flashed and darted as men broke into a run.

In the deeper shadows men in grey coats—Russian soldiers?—suddenly loomed, then disappeared. Or was it only imagination? Confusion began to escalate into near-panic. Orders were called, and countermanded. Voices were raised irately.

Russell rode on, mounting the ridge which lay between the allied headquarters and the small town of Inkerman at the mouth of the River Tchernaya. Immediately he found himself on the edge of 'the bloodiest struggle ever witnessed since war cursed the earth'.

Huge numbers of Russians were pouring out of Sebastopol and sweeping down on the British lines, in one vast attempt to break the siege.

November 5th, 1854. The allies were caught completely by surprise. Little had been done to strengthen their position since the Battle of Balaklava, ten days before. Back in London, Delane had called, in *The Times*'s editorial columns, for reinforcements to be sent out to the Crimea, but nothing had been done.

And so began . . .

⊙ . . . a series of dreadful deeds of daring, of sanguinary hand-to-hand fights, of despairing rallies, of desperate assaults—in glens and valleys, in brushwood glades and remote dells . . . ⊙

Once again, Russell found his own position one for which there were no rules, no precedents—and very little security of any kind.

⊙ Here I was in a raging battle—no place where men were not falling, where death was not flying on leaden or iron wings. And let me say, it is—for a man who has no orders to obey, no orders to give, to find himself under fire, a strange position—very uncomfortable to say the least of it.

He cannot, if he cares for his own good opinion or for

Russians advancing at Inkerman

those around him, gallop off . . . If a bullet finds its billet
in his body corporate, he knows that the general verdict
will be 'Serve him right, what business had he to get in the
way?'.

If a correspondent is involved in the thick of a battle he
has to consider whether he ought to trust to his imagination
for his facts, or whether he will run the chance of dying
without emolument or glory, present or posthumous, and
depriving his editor of 'any account of the proceedings'. ⊙

Some of his fears, at least, were allayed by the letter
written about this time by John Walter, the proprietor of
The Times, which told him that £500 had been invested in his
name, for the benefit of his children. Just as encouraging,
perhaps, were the words which went before, assuring him
that:

⊙ If the glory of the British Army has shone with undiminished lustre during this memorable struggle, it may safely be added that on no occasion have the arduous and even dangerous duties of 'Our own Correspondent' been performed with greater ability or success . . .

Whatever privations you have yourself encountered in the discharge of these duties, it must be some consolation to you to reflect that your light is not hid under a bushel, but that your graphic descriptions of the grand and terrific scenes you have witnessed are read by hundreds of thousands with the same intense interest, and will probably be as imperishable as the memory of the deeds which they recount. ⊙

Perhaps these prophetic words did help to buoy him up when the worst of the danger threatened—and he came very close to death more than once on that memorable day.

Writing privately to Delane when the Inkerman battle was over, he reported:

⊙ I gave Eber a shakedown the night before and we were together nearly all day and two very narrow escapes we both had—once when a shell burst. A 10-incher, and the fragments turned up the ground around us and threw dirt all over Eber. I was in front of him and a piece about the size of a teacup whistled past my head as I lay on the ground, within an inch of my hand . . .

There was no safety anywhere except at Headquarters, and there of course one could not stay on such an occasion . . . ⊙

Other correspondents from London were less conscientious. Russell goes on to report . . .

⊙ The *Morning Herald* correspondent lives on board the *Caradoc*, and comes on shore now and then after a battle to view the ground. The *Daily News* lives on board another ship and never I believe comes on shore at all . . . ⊙

It was not only in the bloody hand-to-hand fighting that men died that day close to Inkerman.

⊙ One of the first things the Russians did, when a break

in the fog enabled them to see the camp of the Second Division, was to open fire on the tents with round shot and large shell, and tent after tent was blown down, torn to pieces or sent into the air, while the men engaged in camp duties, and the unhappy horses tethered up in the lines, were killed or mutilated . . . ◉

But for most of the time fog and drizzling rain continued to obscure the view, and as the turmoil and confusion increased . . .

◉ Our generals could not see where to go. They could not tell where the enemy were—from what side they were coming, nor where they were coming to. In darkness, gloom and rain they had to lead our lines through thick scrubby bushes and thorny brakes, which broke our ranks and irritated the men, while every pace was marked by a corpse or man wounded by an enemy whose position was only indicated by the rattle of musketry and the rush of ball and shell. ◉

Sir George Cathcart fell, urging on the 4th Division, with a bullet wound in the head and three bayonet wounds in the body. 'Poor kindly, gallant Colonel Seymour', who was also wounded, got down from his horse to aid his chief, but the enemy rushed in on them and when the 4th Division fell back, leaving five hundred of their number behind, both men lay dead, side by side.

Russell's old adversary, Sir George Brown, fell wounded too, hit by a shot which went through his arm and struck his side.

◉ I saw with regret his pale and sternly composed face, as he was borne by me on a litter early in the day, his white hair flickering in the breeze, for I knew we had lost the services of a good soldier that day. ◉

About half past nine Lord Raglan and his staff assembled on a knoll, in the vain hope of getting a glimpse of the battle raging below them.

⊙ A shell came right among the staff—it exploded in Captain Somerset's horse, ripping him open; then it struck down Captain Gordon's horse and killed him at once, and then blew away General Strangway's leg so that it hung by a shred of flesh and bit of cloth from the skin. The poor old General never moved a muscle of his face. He said merely, in a gentle voice, 'Will anyone be kind enough to lift me off my horse?'

He was taken down and laid on the ground, while his life-blood ebbed fast, and at last he was carried to the rear. ⊙

The Russians seemed to be making a determined effort to 'pick off' mounted officers; but the men suffered heavily as well. When the second division was assembled in the rear of their camp after the fighting it numbered only three hundred out of a total of almost 3,000.

Altogether the British forces were heavily outnumbered.

⊙ For three long hours about 8,500 British infantry contended against at least four times their number. No wonder that at times they were compelled to retire. But they came to the charge again. The admirable devotion of the officers, who knew they were special objects of attack, can never be too highly praised.

The rolling of musketry, the crash of steel, the pounding of the guns was deafening, and the Russians as they charged up the heights yelled like demons.

They advanced, halted, advanced again, received and returned a close and deadly fire. This disproportion of numbers was, however, too great—our men were exhausted with slaying. But at last came help. About ten o'clock a body of French infantry appeared on our right—a joyful sight to our struggling regiments . . .

Their trumpets sounded above the din of battle, and when we watched their eager advance right on the flank of the enemy we knew the day was won.

Some of the horses killed at Inkerman

Assailed in front by our men—broken by the impetuosity of our charge, renewed again and again—attacked by the French infantry, sometimes led on by English officers, on the right, and by artillery all along the line—the Russians began to retire, and at twelve o'clock they were driven pellmell down the hill towards the valley, where pursuit would have been madness as the roads were all covered by their artillery. They left mounds of dead behind them.

At twelve o'clock the battle of Inkerman seemed to have been won, but the day, which had cleared up about eleven, so as to enable us to see the enemy, again became obscured. Rain and fog set in, and as we could not pursue the Russians, who were retiring under the shelter of their artillery, we formed in front of our lines, and the enemy, covering his retreat by bodies of horse on the slopes, near the Careening Bay, and by a tremendous fire of artillery, fell back upon the works and retreated, in immense confusion, across the Inkerman Bridge. ⊙

12
Soldiering with the gilding off

November 1854. The carnage had been dreadful. Two days after the battle Russell returned to the field.

⊙ The British and the French, many of whom had been murdered by the Russians as they lay wounded, wore terrible frowns on their faces, with which the agonies of death had clad them. Some in their last throes had torn up the earth in their hands, and held the grass between their fingers up towards heaven.

All the men who exhibited such signs of pain had been bayoneted; the dead men who lay with an eternal smile on their lips had been shot. But the wounded, for two days they had lain where the hand and the ball had felled them. There were very few, it is true, but it was towards noon on the 7th ere the last of our soldiers had been found in his lair and carried to the hospital.

The Russians, groaning and palpitating as they lay around, were far more numerous. Some were placed together in heaps, that they might be the more readily removed. Others glared upon you from the bushes with the ferocity of wild beasts, as they hugged their wounds.

Some implored, in an unknown tongue, but in accents not to be mistaken, water, or succour; holding out their mutilated and shattered limbs, or pointing to the track of the lacerating ball.

The sullen, angry scowl of some of these men was fearful. Fanaticism and immortal hate spake through their angry eyeballs, and he who gazed on them with pity and compassion could at last (unwillingly) understand how these men would in their savage passion kill the wounded and fire on the conqueror who, in his generous humanity, had aided them as he passed. It was a relief to see that their arms were broken—that their cartridges were lying opened in heaps on the ground.

Litter-bearers, French and English, dotted the hillside, toiling painfully up with a heavy burden for the grave, or with some subject for the doctor's care, hunting through the bushes for the dead and dying.

Our men had acquired a shocking facility in their diagnosis. A body was before you; there was a shout, 'Come here, boys, I see a Russian!' (or 'a Frenchman', or 'one of our fellows!')

One of the party advanced, raised the eyelid if it was closed, peered into the eye, shrugged his shoulders, saying quietly, 'He's dead, he'll wait' and moved back to the litter. Others pulled the feet, and arrived at equally correct conclusions by that process.

The dead were generally stripped of all but their coats. The camp followers and blackguards from Balaklava, and seamen from the ships, anxious for trophies, carried off all they could take from the field.

At particular spots men were seen busy at work. Groups were digging away all along the hillside, forty or fifty yards apart. On going over, you found them around a yawning trench, thirty feet in length by twenty feet in breadth and six feet in depth, at the bottom of which, in every conceivable attitude, lay packed together with exceeding art some thirty or forty corpses.

The grave-diggers stood chatting on the mounts by the sides, waiting for the arrival of some bearers to complete the number of dead. They speculated on the appearance of the body which was being borne towards them.

'It's Corporal —— of the —th, I think,' says one.

'No, it's my rear rank man! I can see his red hair plain enough . . .' and so on.

At last the number in the trench was completed. The bodies were packed as closely as possible. Some had upraised arms, in the attitude of taking aim; their legs stuck up through the mould as it was thrown upon them; others were bent and twisted into shapes like rag dolls. Inch after inch the earth rose upon them.

For about one mile and a half in length by half a mile in depth, the hillside offered such sights as these. Upwards of 2,000 Russians had been buried by these men. The carnage at the Alma did not present anything like the scene round the Sandbag Battery, which was placed on a steep descent towards the Tchernaya. The piles of dead here were frightful. Upwards of 1,200 dead and dying Russians laid behind and around and in front of it, and many a bearskin cap and tall English Grenadier were mixed with frequent corpses of French Chasseur and infantry soldiers . . .

The men resembled those we met at the Alma, and were clad and armed in the same way. We saw no infantry with helmets, however, and our soldiers were disappointed to find the Russians had, in most cases, come out without their knapsacks.

Their persons were very cleanly, and the whiteness of their faces and of their feet were remarkable. Few had socks on and the marauders, who ever prowl over a battlefield, had removed their boots whenever they were worth taking.

Our soldiers and sailors, as well as the French, looked out with avidity for a good pair of Russian boots and were quite adept in fitting themselves to a nicety by their simple mode of measurement—viz, placing their feet against those of the dead men . . .

It was again asserted, and I sincerely believe with truth, that the dying and wounded Russians killed many of our men as they passed on towards the front against the retreating enemy. For this reason our soldiers smashed the stock and bent the barrel of nearly every firelock they came across.

Some, however, carried bundles of them off the field . . . which they sold to the captains and soldiers of merchantmen, or to those who are anxious for mementoes of the fight. Medals, ribands, the small brass crucifixes and pictures of saints, and charms found upon the dead, were also in great request. The field was visited by shoals of people from Balaklava every day. ⊙

This scrabbling for loot was a triumph of greed over fear—and even discretion—for the Russians, suspicious that the allies were choosing new sites for batteries under cover of burying the dead, fired off regular salvoes from their ships in harbour. Russell himself was almost killed by one shell which tore a hole in his coat.

As always, in victory or defeat, Russell was quick to remind his readers back in England of the stalwart qualities of the British soldier—and the appalling difficulties under which he was fighting in the Crimea.

⊙ If it is considered that the soldiers who met these furious columns of the Czar were the remnants of three British divisions, which scarcely numbered 8,500 men; that they were hungry and wet, and half-famished; that they were men belonging to a force which was generally 'out of bed' four nights out of seven; which had been enfeebled by sickness, by severe toil, sometimes for twenty-four hours at a time without relief of any kind; that among them were men who had within a short time previously lain out for forty-eight hours in the trenches at a stretch—it will be readily admitted that never was a more extraordinary contest maintained by our army since it acquired a reputation in the world's history. ⊙

Once again, though, nothing had been won by either side,

although in one sense the Russians—apparently the losers—had gained their objective. The allies were in even less of a state now to attack Sebastopol, and winter was almost upon them.

Ironically, only a matter of days before the Battle of Inkerman, Lord Raglan had at last persuaded the French that an assault on the great fortress was essential; the date had even been fixed, November 7th, and an appointment had been made for the generals to meet to discuss final details—on the 5th, the very day the Russians launched their attack. His Lordship had pressed for the action because he felt the army could never survive a winter in the Crimea . . .

Russell himself was worried about the most basic necessities, and of conditions among the officers and men in the field he wrote indignantly:

◉ The oldest soldiers never witnessed nor heard of a campaign in which general officers were obliged to live out in tents on the open field, for the want of a roof to cover them, and generals who passed their youth in the Peninsular war, and who had witnessed a good deal of fighting since that time in various parts of the world, were unanimous in declaring that they never knew or read of a war in which the officers were exposed to such hardships.

They landed without anything but what they could carry, and they marched beside their men, slept by them, fought by them, and died by them, undistinguished from them in any respect except by the deadly epaulet and swordbelt, which have cost so many lives.

The survivors were often unable to get their things from on board ship. They laid down at night in the clothes which they wore during the day; many delicately-nurtured youths never changed shirt or shoes for weeks together, and they were deprived of the use of water for ablution, except to a very limited extent . . .

Guardsmen, who were 'the best style of men' in the Parks, turned out in coats and trousers and boots all seams and patches, torn in all directions, and mended with more vigour than neatness, and our smartest cavalry and line men were models of ingenious sewing and stitching. The men could not grumble at old coats, boots, or shoes when they saw their officers no better off than themselves . . . ◉

Russell himself was thoroughly disillusioned with warfare. It was only a matter of months since he had started out, full of sound and glory—but the drums were muffled now, and the trumpets discordant.

◉ We have out here 'soldiering with the gilding off', and many a young gentleman would be for ever cured of his love of arms if he could but see one day's fighting and have one day's parade of the men who do it.

Fortunate it is for us that we have a youth on whom to rely, and that there are in old England men 'who delight in war' and who will be ever ready to incur privation, danger, and death at her summons.

As to young ladies suffering from 'scarlet fever' . . . who are forever thinking of heroes and warriors, singing of champions, of 'crowning conquerors' brows with flowers' and wishing for 'Arab steeds and falchions bright'—if they could but for one instant have stood beside me and gazed into one of the pits where some 30 'clods of the valley' all covered with scarlet and blue cloth, with lace and broidery, and blood, were lying side by side, and staring up to heaven with their sightless orbs as they were about to be consigned to the worm, they would feel the horrors of their hero worship, and would join in prayer for the advent of that day—if come it ever may—when war shall be no more, and when the shedding of blood shall cease. ◉

But the worst was only just beginning.

13

That blackguard, Mr Russell

November 1854. On November 14th, during the early hours of the morning it began once more to rain.

⊙ For about an hour I had been in a listless state between waking and sleeping, listening to the pelting of the rain against the fluttering canvas of the tent, or dodging the streams of water which flowed underneath it, saturating our blankets and collecting on the mackintosh sheets in pools.

The sound of the rain, its heavy beating on the earth, had become gradually swallowed up by the noise of the rushing of the wind over the common, and by the flapping of the tents as they rocked more violently beneath its force.

Gradually the sides of the canvas, which were tucked in under big stones to secure them, began to rise and flutter, permitting the wind to enter playfully and drive before it sheets of rain right into one's face; the pegs began to indicate painful indecision and want of firmness of purpose.

The glimpses afforded of the state of affairs outside, by the lifting of the tent walls, were little calculated to produce a spirit of resignation to the fate which threatened our frail shelter. The ground had lost its character of solidity, and pools of mud marked the horse and cattle-tracks in front of the tents.

Mud—and nothing but mud—flying before the wind and drifting as though it were rain, covered the face of the earth as far as it was visible. ⊙

The hurricane which was to devastate the allies' camp was beginning to gather force . . .

⊙ At every fresh blast the pole of the tent played and bent like a salmon-rod; the canvas tugged at the ropes to pull them up, and the pegs yielded gently. A startling crack! I looked at my companions, who seemed determined to shut out all sound and sense by piling as many clothes as they could collect over their heads.

A roar of wind, and the pole bent till the fatal 'crack' was heard again.

'Get up, Doctor! Up with you. . . . The tent is coming down!'

A harsh screaming sound, increasing in vehemence as it approached struck us with horror. As it passed along we heard the snapping of tent-poles and the sharp crack of timber and canvas.

On it came—'a mighty and a strong wind' . . . the pole broke off short in the middle as if it were glass, and in an instant we were pressed down and half stifled by the heavy folds of the wet canvas, which beat us about the head with the greatest fury.

Half breathless and blind, I struggled for the door. Such a sight met the eye!

The whole headquarters' camp was beaten flat to the earth, and the unhappy occupants were rushing through the mud in all directions in chase of their effects and clothes, as they strove to make their way to the roofless and windowless barns and stables for shelter . . . ⊙

Amid the misery and the tragedy there were moments of comedy which Russell did not miss.

⊙ Next to our tent was the marquee of Captain de Morel. It lay fluttering on the ground and as I looked, the canvas seemed animated by some great internal convulsion —a mimic volcano appeared to be opening beneath it and its folds assumed the most fantastic shapes . . .

The phenomenon was speedily accounted for by the apparition of the gallant owner fighting his way out desperately

141

against the wind which was bent on tearing his very scanty covering from his person . . .

Captain Chetwode was tearing through the rain and dirt like a maniac after a cap which he fancied was his own—and which he found, after a desperate run, to be his sergeant's!

The air was filled with blankets, hats, greatcoats, little coats, and even tables and chairs. Mackintoshes, quilts, india-rubber tubs, bed-clothes, sheets of tent canvas, went whirling like leaves in the gale towards Sebastopol. The shingle roofs of the outhouses were torn away and scattered over the camp, and a portion of the roof of Lord Raglan's house was carried off to join them.

The barns and commissariat-sheds were laid bare at once, large arabas, or wagons, which stood close to us were overturned; men and horses were knocked down and rolled over and over; the ambulance wagons were turned topsy-turvy.

The ridges, the plains and undulating tracts between the ravines, so lately smiling in the autumn sun, with row after row of neat white tents, was bare and desolate, the surface turned into sticky mud as black as ink . . .

The face of the country was covered with horses which had torn away from the pickets. Nearly one half of our cavalry horses broke loose. ◉

Those wounded in the Battle of Inkerman were, perhaps, most wretched of all. Their shelter was as vulnerable as the rest and they 'had to bear the inclemency of the weather as best they could'.

Guard tents were down, the officers of the guard fled to the commissariat stores; but 'inside the commissariat yard, overturned carts, dead horses and groups of shivering men were seen—not a tent was left standing'.

It is possible to read just a hint of satisfaction in Russell's report that:

◉ Our generals' marquees were as incapable of resisting

the hurricane as the bell-tents of the common soldiers. Lord Lucan was seen for hours sitting up to his knees in sludge amid the wreck of his establishment, meditative as Marius amid the ruins of Carthage. ◉

And there is no denying the gleam of impish pleasure in:

◉ Lord Cardigan was sick on board his yacht in the harbour of Balaklava. Sir George Brown was lying wounded on board the *Agamemnon*; Sir de Lacy Evans, sick and shaken, was on board the *Sanspareil* in Balaklava; General Bentinck, wounded, was on board the *Caradoc* on his way to England. The Duke of Cambridge, sick and depressed, was passing an anxious time in the *Retribution*, in all the horrors of that dreadful scene at sea. In fact all the generals and colonels and officers in the field were just as badly off as the meanest private. ◉

Unfortunately the battering of the fleet did not only mean discomfort for the generals. Vast quantities of vital stores were lost which, added to the losses after the Battle of Balaklava, were to spell final disaster for the allies that terrible winter.

About mid-day on the following morning the wind, which had been blowing from the south-west, backed towards the west and became much colder. At first the rain turned to sleet; then came a snow-storm which 'clothed the desolate landscape in white, till the tramp of men seamed it with trails of black mud'.

There seemed no end to the blows fate had in store for the poor wretches still reeling from the savagery of the Russian attack at Inkerman. During a temporary lull attempts were made to re-pitch the tents. They were 'but sorry resting places' for they 'flapped about so much and admitted such quantities of snow, rain and filth from outside that it was quite out of the question to sleep in them'.

Russell and his companions abandoned theirs as hopeless

and made for the barn used as a stable for the horses of
Lord Raglan's escort of the 8th Hussars.

They 'waded across the sea of nastiness which lay between
us and it, tacked against several gusts, fouled one or two
soldiers in a different course, grappled with walls and angles
of outhouses, nearly foundered in big horse holes, bore
sharply up round a corner and anchored at once in the
stable . . .'

They were not the only ones who had the idea of seeking
shelter in the barn.

⊙ What a scene it was! The officers of the escort were
crouching over some embers of a wood fire; along the walls
were packed some thirty or forty horses and ponies, shivering with cold and kicking and biting with spite and bad
humour . . .

Soldiers of different regiments crowded about the warm
corners, and Frenchmen of all arms, and a few Turks, joined
in the brotherhood of misery, lighted their pipes at the
scanty fire, and sat close for mutual comfort.

The wind blew savagely through the roof, and through
chinks in the mud walls and window-holes. The building was
a mere shell, as dark as pitch, and smelt as it ought to do—
an honest, unmistakable stable—improved by a dense pack
of moist and mouldy soldiers . . .

The storm, from half past six o'clock till late in the day,
passed over the camp with the fury of Azrael, vexing and
buffeting every living thing and tearing to pieces all things
inanimate.

We sat in the dark till night set in—not a soul could stir
out. Nothing could be heard but the howling of the wind,
the yelping of wild dogs driven into the enclosures, and the
shrill neighings of terrified horses.

At length a candle-end was stuck into a horn lantern, to
keep it from the wind—a bit of ration pork and some rashers
of ham, done over the wood fire furnished an excellent

dinner, which was followed by a glass or horn of hot water
and rum, then a pipe, and as it was cold and comfortless, we
got to bed—a heap of hay on the stable floor, covered with
our clothes and thrown close to the heels of a playful grey
mare . . . ⊙

The morning of November 15th dawned cold—the mountain sides and hilltops were covered with snow—but the
sky was brighter, and in spite of ankle-deep mud the men
cheered up at the sight of the sun.

Rumours about the devastation in Balaklava began to
trickle in, and Russell set out to see for himself the full extent of the damage.

⊙ The roads were mere quagmires. Dead horses and
cattle were scattered all over the country, and here and there
a sad little procession, charged with the burden of some
inanimate body, might be seen wending its way slowly
towards the hospital marquees, which had been again
pitched. ⊙

As he drew near the town the signs of destruction grew
worse.

⊙ At the narrow neck of the harbour two or three large
boats were lying, driven inland several yards from the
water; the shores were lined with trusses of hay which had
floated out of the wrecks outside the harbour, and masts
and spars of all sizes were stranded on the beach or floated
about among the shipping.

The condition of Balaklava at that time is utterly indescribable. The narrow main street was a channel of mud,
through which horses, wagons, camels, mules and soldiers
and sailors, and men of all nations—English, French, Turks,
Arabs, Egyptians, Italians, Maltese, Tartars, Greeks, Bul-
garians and Spaniards—scrambled and plunged, and jostled,
and squattered along; while strange oaths, yells and un-
earthly cries of warning or expostulation filled the air, combined with the noise of the busy crowds around the sutlers'

stores, and with the clamorous invitations of the vendors to their customers.

Many of the houses were unroofed, several had been destroyed altogether and it was quite impossible to find quarters in the place . . . ⊙

Stunned as they were by this disaster, the allies had no peace. The siege went on relentlessly. Something of the desperation they must all have felt at this time crept into the brief dispatch Russell wrote a few days after the storm, on November 18th.

⊙ The mail leaves to-day for England. There is no news of any kind. The siege drags its slow length along day after day till one is out of patience with it.

The sensation of weariness produced by this slow cannonade is indescribable. It must be something like that which would be experienced by a man who lived in a house where an amateur played on the big drum in the drawing-room morning, noon, and night. ⊙

Winter 1854/55. The bitter disappointment and frustration among the generals both before and after the disaster of Inkerman caused them to look around for explanations, excuses—and a whipping boy. They did not need to look far.

'That blackguard Mr Russell of *The Times*', as one infuriated officer described him, was 'as good as a Russian spy', with his precise descriptions—not only of the weakness of the British army, and its lack of equipment and ammunition (which all-but invited the Russians to attack)—but of the location of different regiments, and even a powder mill.

The Prince Consort described him as a 'miserable scribbler', and Sidney Herbert fervently hoped that the Army would lynch him. Lord Clarendon, the Foreign Secretary, thought that 'three pitched battles gained would not repair the mischief done by Mr Russell' (though he changed his mind before many months had passed).

Russell himself claimed that by the time his dispatches reached London, were printed and circulated, the news he sent was stale and of little value to the enemy. After the war was over one of the Russian commanders wrote to tell him that he had 'learned nothing from them that he had not known already'.

◉ There was not a single man in the camp [Russell protested] who could put his hand on his heart and declare he believed that one single casualty had been caused to us by information communicated to the enemy by me or any other newspaper correspondent.

The only thing the partisans of misrule could allege was that I did not make things pleasant to the authorities, and that, amid the filth and starvation, and deadly stagnation of the camp, I did not go about 'babbling of green fields', of present abundance, and of prospects of victory. ◉

But there is no denying that the cumulative effect of reports of sickness, scarcity of equipment, exhaustion, muddle and mismanagement must have had a cheering effect on the Russians over a period, and perhaps 'screwed their courage to the sticking place' when otherwise it might have faltered. (It was at the time claimed that copies of *The Times* reached Sebastopol before they reached British headquarters; and that the gist of Russell's reports was telegraphed to the Russians long before this.)

Individual misfortunes laid at his door are less convincing:

◉ The Russians left off shooting at our camp entirely but Mr Russell must needs go put in his paper that the balls had reached us. We saw it in *The Times* a fortnight ago and at the moment I saw it I said that as soon as the Russians heard it we should be shot at again, and sure enough the night before last, just as we were at dinner, they commenced their evening's performance. ◉

This, surely, stretches the long arm of coincidence almost

to breaking point.

In any case, what was Russell to do? He protested that his job was to describe what he saw, as he saw it; to inform his Editor, and the British public, of what was going on. That it was the responsibility of those at home to censor what he wrote, if necessary.

But Delane was first and foremost a newspaper man, with a newspaperman's instinct for a good story, and a circulation to keep up. *The Times* had by now achieved a reputation for the brilliance of its war-reporting; there was hardly a literate man or woman in Britain who did not follow Russell's breathtaking dispatches. It was asking a lot of any editor to expect him to refrain from printing anything which would catch his readers' eyes and get them talking.

Besides, like Russell, he firmly believed that government and army mismanagement should be exposed. Why, after all, should those in authority get away, literally, with murder under the cloak of 'security'?

As a final absolution from direct responsibility Delane claimed that an offer had been made to the Duke of Newcastle (Secretary of State for War) 'to suppress not only all that could possibly assist the enemy in our correspondence from the Crimea, but also all the intelligence of naval and military movements here which we believed, and still believe, to be of much greater importance. (Early in the war Lord Hardinge, then Master-General of the Ordnance, had himself sent Delane exact details of regiments sailing to the Crimea, with their precise strength!) The Duke did not think this necessary but our offer and his reply remain, and can be produced.'

Russell's personal attacks on individual high-ranking officers charged with the conduct of the war were perhaps less defensible, though it would have been difficult for him to write as he did without apportioning blame.

Perhaps if they had taken him into their confidence, and explained the necessity for silence on certain subjects, a much happier relationship might have been established; and Russell might (though only might) have suppressed some of the information he poured out in a ceaseless stream.

Lord Raglan was especially bitter about the publication of military secrets he himself was at great pains to protect; and to a lesser extent about Russell's attacks on himself. He died before the outcome of the Crimean War was decided, and there are those who believe that *The Times*'s great correspondent in the Crimea contributed to the final breakdown in his health.

As early as the Battle of the Alma Russell gave his frank opinion of the Commander-in-Chief.

⊙ That Lord Raglan was brave as a hero of antiquity, that he was kind to his friends and to his staff, that he was unmoved under fire, and unaffected by personal danger, that he was noble in manner, gracious in demeanour, of dignified bearing, I am ready to admit; that he had many and great difficulties to contend with I believe; but that this brave and gallant nobleman had lost, if he ever possessed, the ability to conceive and execute large military plans—and that he had lost, if he ever possessed, the faculty of handling great bodies of men, I am firmly persuaded. ⊙

Perhaps no one—not even the great Duke of Wellington himself—could have overcome the fatal Crimean mixture of bad luck, unfavourable weather, inexperienced officers and men; and lack of support from the Government at home. There is no doubt that Lord Raglan did everything in his power to save his army—working far into the night, every night, on unending 'desk work'. It was just not enough. Like King Canute, he sat amid a rising tide of problems and paper, and was unable to stem the flow.

Given the choice he would probably have excluded the Press altogether from the field, as his former chief had during the Peninsular Campaigns, but he had not Wellington's strength of character and it is doubtful whether people of the calibre of Delane would have taken much notice anyway. Newspapers were a good deal stronger in 1854 than they had been in 1809—and no one quite like Russell had appeared before. No rules existed to control him.

It is difficult, too, to see what good would have come of such an exclusion. The 'exposures' by Russell and his colleagues may not have done much to win the war, but they did a very great deal to change conditions for the army in later years; to unseat an incompetent Government and stir the consciences of the complacent middle-class in England.

There had been few, if any, in the past to act as public champion of the ordinary soldier, who was generally looked upon as slightly less than human—almost incapable of feeling heat, cold, pain or discomfort. Russell's ruthless and lively descriptions of his hardships and agony, the homely details of his everyday life, gave faces to the hitherto faceless masses; turned regiments and battalions into legions of Billys and Jacks and Joes and Alberts—men whose skin burned in the sun and turned blue with cold.

If the great British public had seen its soldiers at all, it had seen them swaggering about the garrison towns in colourful uniforms, reasonably well-fed by the standards of the time, and certainly better-dressed than the great majority. It needed Russell to show the other side of the picture.

14
All we can do is protest

Winter 1854/55. As winter closed over the Crimea things got worse. Many of the ships in Balaklava harbour devastated by the hurricane had been loaded with vital stores. At least twenty days' supply of provender for all the horses and many of the men was lost.

⊚ . . . [The army] worn out by night work, by vigil in rain and storm, by hard labour in the trenches, found themselves suddenly reduced to short allowance. . . . For nine days, with very few exceptions, no issue of tea, coffee, or sugar, to the troops took place . . . ⊚

The gale was not the only cause of the shortages—the difficulties of moving supplies about was a contributory factor. Russell as usual was quick to draw attention to the lack of foresight on the part of authority.

⊚ But though there was a cause, there was no excuse for the privations to which the men were exposed. We were all told that when the bad weather set in, the country roads would be impassable. Still the fine weather was allowed to go by, and the roads were left as the Tartar carts had made them, though the whole face of the country was covered thickly with small stones which seemed expressly intended for road metal . . .

As I understood, it was suggested by the officers of the Commissariat Department that they should be allowed to form depots of food, corn and forage, as a kind of reserve at the headquarters of the different divisions; but instead of being permitted to carry out this excellent idea, their carts, arabas, wagons and horses were, after a few days' work in forming these depots, taken for the use of the siege operations . . . Consequently, the magazines at headquarters were small, and were speedily exhausted when the daily supplies from Balaklava could no longer be procured. ⊚

As if all this was not enough, cholera broke out again towards the end of November. Balaklava, never suitable as a base for an army the size of the allies', became the scene of hideous desolation.

⊚ . . . Words could not describe its filth, its horror, its

151

hospitals, its burials, its dead and dying Turks, its crowded lanes, its noisome sheds, its beastly purlieus, or its decay. All the pictures ever drawn of plague and pestilence . . . fall short of individual 'bits' of disease and death, which anyone might see in half-a-dozen places during half an hour's walk in Balaklava.

In spite of all our efforts, the dying Turks have made of every lane and street a cess-pit, and the forms of human suffering which meet the eye at every turn, and once were wont to shock us, have now made us callous, and ceased even to attract passing attention.

By raising up the piece of matting or coarse rug which hangs across the doorway of some miserable house, from within which you hear wailings and cries of pain and prayers to the Prophet, you will see in one spot and in one instant a mass of accumulated woes that will serve you with night-mares for a lifetime. The dead, laid out as they died, are lying side by side with the living, and the latter present a spectacle beyond all imagination.

The commonest accessories of a hospital are wanting; there is not the least attention paid to decency or cleanliness —the stench is appalling—the fœtid air can barely struggle out to taint the atmosphere, save through the chinks in the walls and roofs, and, for all I can observe, these men die without the least effort being made to save them.

There they lie, just as they were let gently down on the ground by the poor fellows, their comrades, who brought them on their backs from the camp with the greatest tender-ness, but who are not allowed to remain with them.

The sick appear to be tended by the sick, and the dying by the dying . . . ◉

Meanwhile on the battlefield stalemate had been reached. The Russians made very little attempt to drive the allies from their entrenched positions, and the allies were in no state to make a determined assault on Sebastopol. An occasional half-hearted burst of gunfire, an occasional reconnaissance, did nothing to change the situation.

December dragged its weary, ice-cold, feet across the land. Men shivered in their tents, now virtually useless: 'so long exposed to the blazing Bulgarian sun, and continually drenched by torrents of rain' they 'let the wet through like sieves'.

A great deal of the warm winter clothing belatedly sent out from England had either gone down with the *Prince* on the night of the storm, or burnt in another ill-fated ship off Constantinople. Even that which survived these two disasters was, through sheer carelessness, ruined. Russell saw:

⊙ . . . several lighters full of warm greatcoats etc. for the men, lying a whole day in the harbour of Balaklava beneath a determined fall of rain and snow.

There was no one to receive them when they were sent to the shore, or rather no one would receive them without orders. In fact we are ruined by etiquette, and by service regulations. No one would take responsibility upon himself even to save the lives of hundreds . . .

We are cursed by a system of requisitions, orders, and memos which is enough to depress an army of scriveners. . . ⊙

And while the clerks scribbled in their account books, sent each other notes in official jargon—in the Crimea and in London—men shivered and coughed and died.

Charcoal stoves which produced a little warmth in the tents also gave out deadly fumes, so that those who did not die from cold or cholera, suffocated.

The allies began to fight among themselves over the meagre supplies which did reach the camps. The French-Algerian troops—brave fighters in the field, but unfortunately equally belligerent towards their comrades in the face of starvation—began to raid the British food carts:

⊙ Let an araba once stick, or break a wheel or an axle and the Zouaves sniffed it out just as vultures detect carrion; in a moment barrels and casks were broken open, the bags of bread ripped up, the contents were distributed and the commissary officer who had gone to seek for help and assistance, on his return found only the tires of the wheels and a few splinters of wood left . . . ◉

Christmas came, and New Year: the 'festive' season. But there was little to rejoice about in the Crimea, and very little opportunity to express joyful feelings.

◉ At the close of the year there were 3,500 sick in the British camp before Sebastopol, and it was not too much to say that their illness had, for the most part, been caused by hard work in bad weather and by exposure to wet without any adequate protection . . . ◉

There was, in fact, no real need for the men, or officers, to be exposed to the winds, the frost and the snow as they were. As Russell bitterly reported to the people at home, huts had been sent out to house them through the winter. But where were they?

◉ The huts were on board ships in the harbour of Balaklava. Some of these huts, of which we heard so much, were floating about the beach; others had been landed, and now and then I met a wretched pony, knee-deep in mud, struggling on beneath the weight of two thin deal planks, a small portion of one of these huts, which were most probably converted into firewood after lying for some time in the camp, or turned into stabling for officers' horses. ◉

Miraculously Russell remained healthy and vigorous—kept warm, perhaps, by the heat of his indignation. As the early days of 1855 touched frozen fingers to the near-silent battlefields he scribbled busily on, collecting statistics and firing his own kind of ammunition in the direction of London.

◉ The 63rd Regiment had only seven men fit for duty on the 7th January. The 46th had only thirty men fit for duty on the same date. A strong company of the 90th had been reduced by the week's severity to fourteen file in a few days, and that regiment, though considered very healthy, lost fifty men by death in a fortnight. ◉

The entire landscape was now covered in snow. Stores had to be man-handled the five miles up from Balaklava, and the white blanket was 'seamed and marked by lines of men and horses carrying up provisions'. At night:

◉ Hundreds of men had to go into the trenches with no covering but their greatcoats, and no protection for their feet but their regimental shoes. The trenches were two and three feet deep with mud, snow, and half-frozen slush.

Many when they took off their shoes were unable to get their swollen feet into them again and they might be seen bare-footed, hopping along about the camp with the ther-mometer at twenty degrees, and the snow half a foot deep upon the ground . . . ◉

The men who faced these appalling conditions were not even hardened soldiers. So many had died (or deserted) since the allied landing in the Middle East that the army now in the Crimea was—despite the slowness and unwillingness of

Guarding the advance trench during the winter of 1854–55

recruits to join the colours—virtually a complete replacement.

⊙ It consisted of officers, men, and regiments almost new to this campaign. The generation of six months before had passed away; generals, brigadiers, colonels, captains, and men, the well-known faces of Gallipoli, of Scutari, of Varna—ay, even of the bivouac of Bouljanak, had changed; and there was scarcely one of the regiments once so familiar to me which I could then recognise save by its well-known number.

Excepting Lord Raglan, Lord Lucan, and Sir R. England, not one of our generals remained of those who went out originally; the changes among our brigadiers and colonels were almost as great—all removed from the army by wounds, by sickness, or by death. ⊙

January 1855. All through the bitter winter Russell kept up his barrage of reports and dispatches; only the speed of his writing preventing the ink from freezing on his pen. When he was not writing he was out and about, seeing for himself the horrors he wrote about.

⊙ A large number of sick and, I fear, dying men were sent into Balaklava on the 23rd. . . . They formed one of the most ghastly processions that ever poet imagined. . . . With closed eyes, open mouths, and ghastly attenuated faces, they were borne along two and two, the thin stream of breath visible in the frosty air alone showing they were still alive.

One figure was a horror—a corpse, stone dead, strapped upright in its seat, its legs hanging stiffly down, the eyes staring wide open, the teeth set on the protruding tongue, the head and body nodding with frightful mockery of life at each stride of the mule over the broken road . . .

. . . It would have astonished a stranger riding out from Balaklava to the front to have seen the multitudes of dead horses all along the road. In every gully were piles of the remains of these wretched animals, torn to pieces by wild dogs and vultures, and many of the equine survivors of the desperate charge of Balaklava lay rotting away by the side of the cavalry camp . . . ⊙

Many of the carcasses had been skinned by the Turks and French, who used the hides to cover their huts; and 'many suspicious-looking gaps, too, suggestive of horse-steaks' had been cut out of their flanks.

Later in January cold, clear weather brought frost. The surface of the mud roads and tracks hardened and, at least in the early morning and in the evening, the going between camp and Balaklava became a little easier—and the sunshine which turned the tracks into quagmires again during the day at least warmed the creaking joints and shrivelled flesh of the army.

Meanwhile, the 'private war' between Russell and those in authority was intensifying. Both in his dispatches and in private letters to his Editor, he savagely criticised the general conduct of the war, and the Commander-in-Chief's personal shortcomings.

Delane backed him up in his Editorials. Now *The Times*'s increasing middle-class resentment against the privileged few who had ruled England for so long at last had a legitimate outlet.

Delane encouraged officers in the field to write critically to his newspaper. There was no shortage of those willing to work off their discontent in this way. Such men were inevitably accused by their superiors of disloyalty, and this caused yet more dissension among the army in the Crimea; but their letters provided splendid ammunition for Delane, who did not hesitate to use it.

Lord Raglan's retiring nature indirectly added fuel to the fire. Although he did in fact move about the camps far more than was at the time realised, he moved so unobtrusively that many people believed he had left the Crimea altogether, to winter in Malta—or even London.

⊚ Incompetency, lethargy, aristocratic hauteur, official indifference, favour, routine, perverseness and stupidity reign, revel and riot in the Camp before Sebastopol. . . . We say it with extreme reluctance, no-one sees or hears anything of the Commander-in-Chief [*The Times* thundered in December, 1854]. ⊚

But it was not all Raglan's fault—the chain of responsibility stretched all the way back to London, where scores of clerks sat hunched over desks, scribbling, and hundreds of messengers scurried about . . . where everyone *seemed* to be working frantically, but with very little result, since it took eight months to order, dispatch and finally deliver a consignment of hay, for horses dead long ago. A requisition for tents and marquees desperately needed to keep out the snow and frost-laden winds was the subject of inter-office memos and carefully-worded notes throughout the whole of the coldest weather. The unconvincing excuse given for non-delivery was that 'the demand for tents previous to the war being very limited' there was not enough skilled labour available to make them.

There was a mysterious shortage of transport, too, to carry vital supplies, although Britain at that time had the world's largest navy, and owned half the world's merchant ships.

Delane huffed and puffed and breathed fire over 'the aristocracy' which 'was trifling with the safety of the army in the Crimea', and allowing Lord Raglan to take all-too-much of the blame. It was not just Lord Raglan; not just the Army top brass—or even the War Office, though this sprawling, inefficient, department was long out of date. It was the whole system which was at fault, and something would have to be done about it; something radical.

Other newspapers took up the cry. Public indignation increased. Protest meetings were held.

In response to Russell's descriptions of the privations they were suffering collections were taken, and bales and cases of 'comforts' for the soldiers (some wholly unsuitable) were sent out . . . often personally addressed to *The Times*'s Crimean Correspondent.

Russell himself was not forgotten. Readers of the *Dublin Evening Packet*, proud, no doubt, of his Irish ancestry, sent him a box of provisions which included a plum-pudding 'of a size the bore of no gun could accommodate', together with a supply of worsted (wool) . . . 'forced into all possible shapes and combinations that female fingers could contrive on his behoof' . . . a number of well-corked bottles 'kept from breaking by bundles of cigars . . . and the corners . . . occupied by jars of potted meat . . . whilst in the centre of a stout, useful saucepan (and they are at a premium in the Crimea) . . . was wedged a magnificent cheese'.

There were also German sausages and jars of butter, matches, candles, soap, tea, needles and thread and buttons, a tiny medicine chest and some warm socks.

Perhaps the most welcome gift of all to the correspondent, though, was 'a gross of pens, a stone bottle of ink and a ream of paper . . . '

As the new year began, and there was no sign of improvement or activity, *The Times* called for an entire re-organisation of the War Office. On January 25th Delane wrote:

⊙ We wipe our hands of the war under the existing management. . . . All we can do is to protest, and to warn— and that we will not cease to do. ⊙

The Government, in a panic, fought back. One of the pettier reprisals was a threat to withdraw Russell's army rations (described by Russell as: 'A bleeding chunk of flesh, a piece of goaty mutton or tough beef . . . a pound of de-baked bread; a handful of coffee berries; another of brown sugar; a candle of tallow; a measure of rum; now and then a dole of vegetables . . . ').

Grandly Delane replied:

⊙ . . . the full value of every ration shall be repaid, and the churls who represent a generous country shall not have one farthing to charge to the historian of the war.

At the same time we would venture to remind them that the obligation is not all on our side. It was but the other day another correspondent of *The Times* clothed a regiment which had been sent utterly unprovided by the War Department to rot away in the trenches before Sebastopol. ⊙

This was a reference to the fact that Macdonald (later to become Editor of *The Times*) had arranged for flannel underclothes to be supplied to an entire regiment, sent direct from the tropics to the Crimea with no warm clothing.

Delane might also have reminded the Government of the more-than-twenty-thousand pounds his readers had raised to help finance Florence Nightingale and her nurses, now doing wonderful work in the hospital at Scutari.

In the end the battle was won. A Government crisis arose when one Member, a Mr Roebuck, called for an official inquiry into the conditions of the army before Sebastopol . . . 'and the conduct of those Departments of the Government whose duty it had been to minister to the wants of that army'.

He was by no means the only Member who felt this was necessary. His motion was passed by a large majority. Lord Aberdeen resigned and Lord Palmerston became the new Prime Minister, with Lord Panmure as Secretary of State for War.

Later, when the Duke of Newcastle went out to the Crimea, he met Russell, and told him, 'It was you who turned out the Government, Mr Russell.' An exaggeration, perhaps, but there is no doubt that Russell's constant bombardment of heart-rending letters had a good deal to do with the upheaval.

January/February 1855. Back in the Crimea the hard, dry
cold numbed not only the finger-ends but some of the bel-
ligerence of the fighting men. It is hard to feel 'hot under the
collar' towards an enemy when that collar is in shreds, and
the wind is whistling about it; and when that enemy, poor
fellow, is in much the same boat.

As winter proceeded a kind of good fellowship sprang up
between the allies—especially the French—and men on the
Russian outposts. One day:

⊙ . . . a Chasseur had left his belt and accoutrements in
the ruined Cossack picket-house, and naturally gave up all
hope of recovering them, but on his next visit he found them
on the wall untouched. To requite this act of forbearance,
a French soldier, who had taken a Cossack's lance and pistol
which he found leaning against a tree, was ordered to return
them, and leave them in the place in which he had found
them.

The next time the French went out, one of the men left
a biscuit in a cleft stick, beckoning to the Cossacks to come
and eat it. The following day they found a white loaf of
excellent bread stuck on a stick in the same place, with a
note in Russian which was translated in Balaklava, to the
effect that the Russians had plenty of biscuits, and that,
though greatly obliged for that which had been left, they
really did not want it; but if the French had bread to spare
like the sample left in return, it would be acceptable . . . ⊙

Notes on sticks were not the only communication between the two sides.

⊙ The sentries . . . shouted and yelled to each other, and
one day a Russian called out, as the French were retiring for
the day, 'We will see one another again, friends . . . French,
English, Russians . . . we are all friends . . . ' ⊙

L   161

It is a cry common soldiers everywhere have uttered down the years. There were scenes very similar to these in France, sixty years later, during World War One.

Such demonstrations of friendship must have brought a little light into the men's lives. There was little enough else to cheer or comfort anyone during the long, dragging months of early 1855. Scurvy and typhus fever had been added to the list of illnesses rife in the British camps. Many men were so weak that even when it was possible to bring rations to them they were too exhausted to collect them.

'Uniform' had ceased to exist—men wore anything they could find, beg or steal, to keep them warm. There was no telling the difference between men and officers, until the order was given that officers should wear their swords at all times as a mark of rank.

Regimental variations had long since disappeared; it was even difficult to tell which army men belonged to. An English soldier was as likely to be wearing French trousers as those of his own countrymen. Leggings were contrived from sheepskins or horses' hides. Caps were made from blankets or mess-tin covers.

A group of the 47th Foot during the winter of 1854–55, wearing animal-skin coats and caps to keep out the cold

Beards proliferated. Those who could, grew hair all over their faces; but this was of doubtful benefit—in the extreme cold beards sometimes froze solid, and the men could not open their mouths until they had made a fire to thaw them. If, that is, there was any wood to make one.

Men continued to die at a frightening rate. In April 1854 the number of sick in the British Army Expeditionary Force had been 503. In July, at Varna, the number had risen to nearly 7,000. By September it had climbed to 11,693; by November to 16,846. In January 1855, 23,076 soldiers were suffering from some sort of disease.

During that winter seven times more men died from sickness than in action. The plateau on which the British were camped was 'a vast black waste of soddened earth, when it was not covered with snow, dotted with little pools of foul water and seamed by brown coloured streamlets strewn with carcasses of horses'.

Reinforcements continued to arrive, but few could stand up to the arduous conditions. Many fell sick within a few days, and died without seeing action at all. And in spite of the friendliness of individual Russian soldiers, the bombardment of the miserable men in the trenches went on, day and night.

The monotony was one of the hardest things to bear; the endless procession of days 'shut up' as Russell expressed it 'in one dirty little angle of land'.

15

Comforters, mufflers, tracts, potted game and spirits . . .

February/March 1855. Little by little, as February gave way to March, the ice cracked, the snow receded, the daylight hours nibbled away at the black nights. Winter was reluctantly retreating from the Crimea.

The Russians opened up with furious cannonades—the allies replied. Each side sent out sorties, and between the clashes there were brief periods of armistice, for each side to bury its dead. Then the booming of the guns and the cracking of the rifles began again.

The two armies began to creep stealthily towards each other. The French extended their trenches, foot by foot, towards the Malakoff—one of the major fortifications on the Sebastopol walls—and the Russians began to dig new trenches linking their main defences to a fortified hill-position outside the city, known as the Mamelon.

Very soon the whole region between the two encampments was a spider's-web of interlocking ditches.

It was four months since the last great battle—Inkerman—and neither side had won an inch of ground. Neither had anything to show but a growing stock-pile of ammunition, an increasing area of holes in the ground—and hundreds of graves.

The allies had begun to construct a railway up to the heights from Balaklava, which eased the transport of supplies, though by early March it was 'still not large enough for the demands made upon it'. It was, however, a definite and practical action, and there were some signs at least that more

The commencement of the railway at Balaklava early in 1855.
Cars were drawn up first by horses and then by stationary
winding gear. They came down by gravity

efforts were being made by the new Government to improve
the situation.

⊙ Whatever the cause may be [Russell wrote on March
2nd] it is quite evident that an unusual display of energy has
been visible recently in most of the public departments connected with the army.

The word 'must' begins to be heard ... officers are now
told so many guns *must* be in the batteries on such a day and
that such a work *must* be finished by such a time. . . . A
Sanatorium is about to be established on Balaklava heights,
the hospitals are in order, and now (and only now) a *General*
visits the trenches every day, and sees that the men do not
neglect their duty ... ⊙

But the thought of another summer spent in the Crimea
plunged Russell into gloom:

⊙ . . . for the sun's rays will develop fever and pestilence out of the layers of animal matter festering below the surface of the soil as assuredly as they will ripen the ear or quicken the fruit for autumn . . . ⊙

Cheerfulness, however, would keep breaking in. Scene as it was of so much heart-break and ugliness, the Crimea had an undisputed beauty which pointed the contrast even more sharply. The allies even found time, in the lengthening days and warming sunshine, for a little sport.

⊙ The Tchernaya abounds with duck, and some of the officers have little decoys of their own, where they go at night, in spite of the Russians. It is highly exciting sport, for the Russian batteries over Inkerman will assuredly send a round shot or shell at the sportsman if he is seen by their sentries; but even that does not deter them.

In the daytime they adopt the expedient of taking a few French soldiers down with them, who actually, out of love of the thing, and for the chance of a small reward, were only too happy to go out and occupy the attention of the Cossacks in front, while their patrons were engaged in looking after mallard. ⊙

There was horse-racing, 'numerously attended' and (not surprisingly!) 'regarded with much interest by the Cossack pickets at Kamara and on Canrobert's Hill'.

⊙ They evidently thought at first that the assemblage was connected with some military demonstration and galloped about in a state of excitement, but it is to be hoped they got a clearer notion of the real character of the proceedings ere the sport was over . . . ⊙

Other spare-time occupations were even more bizarre. There were dog-hunts—and even man-hunts (with soldiers as the more-or-less willing quarry)—and:

⊙ One of the commonest and most exciting, while it lasts, is the pursuit of a centipede. A small party are sitting in a hut enjoying a frugal and cheerful meal. Suddenly there is an outcry; a man starts up with a face of horror, and with outstretched finger points to a dark insect, all legs and nippers, about six inches long, which is moving rapidly with a tortuous motion along the wall.

At the shout of 'By Jove, there's a centipede!' everyone leaps up shouting 'Where? Where?'

The boldest seize carving-knives or table-forks; the more adroit two sticks wherewith to catch the artful and venemous enemy—and in a moment the centipede, menaced on all sides, glides rapidly into some chink, where he is pursued by fire and match, or is cut into numberless pieces, and ground up beneath vindictive boot-heels . . . ◉

March 1855. The clearing-up of Balaklava, which began with the cold dry winds of February, continued until 'the oldest inhabitant would not have known the place'. Most encouraging of all . . .

◉ The health of the troops was better, mortality and sickness decreased, and the spirits of the men were good.

The cook-house of the 8th Hussars (King's Royal Irish)

Fresh provisions were becoming abundant and supplies of vegetables were to be had for the sick and scurvy-stricken . . . A great quantity of mules and ponies . . . was collected together and lightened the toils of the troops and of the commissariat department. The public and private stores of warm clothing exceeded the demand.

The mortality among the horses ceased, and, though the oxen and sheep sent over to the camps would not have found much favour in Smithfield, they were very grateful to those who had to feed so long on salt junk alone. ⊙

Almost more important than the arrival of fresh provisions was the arrival of a man who was to make better use of them than anyone could have believed possible. Alexis Soyer was one of the most famous chefs of his age, and a remarkable man: interested equally in *haute cuisine* and soup kitchens for the poor. He had been, amongst other things, chef to the Duke of Sutherland, the Duke of Cambridge, the Marquis of Waterford, and Head Chef of the Reform Club. He had also run his own high-class restaurant at the time of the Great Exhibition.

His attention was drawn to the appalling state of the army's food and cooking arrangements when a letter from a soldier appeared in *The Times*, asking M. Soyer to advise the men on how to use their rations. He replied with a few simple recipes—but from that day on began to read Russell's reports more closely, and with mounting horror. On February 2nd, 1855, he wrote again to *The Times*, offering to go to Scutari at his own expense to 'regulate' the hospital kitchens.

Among his multifarious reforms and innovations was a simple field cooking stove which not only rendered the murderous charcoal stoves obsolete, but reduced the amount of fuel needed to cook for a thousand men from thirty-five hundred to three hundred pounds. Unfortunately these did not arrive in numbers until the war was almost over.

The telegraph had also been established between head-

Huts and warm clothing, too late, for the army

quarters and Kadikoi (near Constantinople); the line was ordered to be speedily carried on to Balaklava, and:

⊙ . . . Every material for carrying on a siege—guns, carriages, platforms, powder, shot, shell, gabions, fascines, scaling-ladders—we had in abundance. The artillery force was highly efficient, notwithstanding the large proportion of young gunners. Our engineers, if not quite so numerous as they ought to have been, were active and energetic; and our army must have consisted of nearly 20,000 bayonets, owing to the great number of men discharged from the hospitals, and returned fit for duty, and to the draughts which had been received.

With the exception of the Guards, who were encamped near Balaklava, quite exhausted and reduced to the strength of a company, nearly every brigade in the army could muster many more men than they could have done a month before . . .

. . . what was more, it was beginning to *look* like an army, instead of resembling an armed mob, with sheepskin coats and bread-bag and sand-bag leggings and butchers' fur caps. The weather was too warm for sheepskins, and the red coat was seen once more, and the influence of 'uniform' returned. ⊙

It was typical of everything to do with the Crimean War that when the tide turned, it almost washed the army away on a wave of good things.

⊙ From hunger, unwholesome food and comparative nakedness, the camp was plunged into a sea of abundance, filled with sheep and sheepskins, wooden huts, furs, comforters, mufflers, flannel shirts, tracts, soups, preserved meats, potted game and spirits; but it was, unfortunately, just in proportion as they did not want them that the comforts and even luxuries were showered upon them.

In such weather a tent was as good as—some say better than—a hut. Where were the huts when the snow was on the ground and where was the warm clothing when the cold rains and bitter winds racked the joints? Just where our fresh meat and vegetables were when scurvy and scorbutic dysentery were raging in the canvas cantonment before Sebastopol . . . [Russell commented bitterly]. ⊙

But he did not waste much time on useless recrimination now. Things were getting better all the time. A hut of his own was one of the luxuries he was enjoying. Delane had sent one out from England, and Mr Doyne, a fellow-Irishman providentially in charge of the Army Work Corps, offered to let his men carry it up from Balaklava and erect it in their spare time for 'a small payment'.

Life was still not all roses. For some time he lived in trepidation in case one of his high-ranking enemies should spot the little building and order its removal—especially as less-fortunate officers could be heard grumbling about it from time to time. Surprisingly he was left in peace, and lived in his little house for the rest of the war—only discovering too late that it was well within range of the Russian guns! By the time he left he had a collection of thirteen shells, all of which had fallen around it.

But for all its drawbacks it was a great improvement on earlier resting places. Shortly before its arrival Russell was sleeping:

⊙ . . . in a sunken hut in which a corpse lies buried, with only a few inches of earth between its head and my own. Within a yard and a half of the door of my present abode are the shallow graves of three soldiers, a little earth heaped up loosely over them, mixed with scanty lime, which does not even destroy the rank vegetation that springs out of them.

Nearer still is a large mound—supposed to contain the remains of a camel—rather a large supply of noxious gases; and further away, at the distance of about 180 yards, are the graves of the division, where hundreds of bodies . . . [lie] . . . as close as they can pack.

In front of the hut are two mounds, about ten feet distant, containing the burial offal of the butchers; and on the left are the remains of more camels, and of God knows what beside . . . ⊙

After that, what were a few Russian shells?

As the sun warmed the last of the 'screws' from their joints, the spirits of the men rose . . .

⊙ The voice of song was heard once more in the tents, and the men commenced tuning up their pipes and chanting their old familiar choruses. The railway pushed its iron feelers up the hillside to the camp. Every day the plains and hillsides were streaked with columns of smoke, which marked the spots where fire was destroying heaps of filth and corrupt animal and vegetable matter as sacrifices on the altar of Health . . .

The silence and gloom of despondency had passed with the snows and rains and the deadly lethargy of our last terrible winter. ⊙

The allies were not the only ones to benefit from the improvement in the weather. The Russians were busy, too, strengthening their defences and bringing in more men.

⊙ We heard that a formidable army had assembled around Eupatoria, and it was certain that the country between that town and Sebastopol was constantly traversed by parties of horse and foot, who were sometimes seen from the sea in very great numbers. ⊙

It was, in fact, becoming increasingly clear that the moment for taking Sebastopol with reasonable ease had long ago been lost.

⊙ Had our army marched upon the place on the 25th September*, it would have fallen almost without resistance. A Russian officer, who was taken prisoner some time before, and who knew the state of the city well, declared that he could not account for our 'infatuation' in allowing the Russians to throw up works and regain heart, when we could have walked into the place, unless under the supposition that the hand of the Almighty was in it, and that He had blinded the vision and perverted the judgement of our generals. ⊙

Throughout the early spring reconnaissance patrols, bombardments, raids and counter-raids, and brief truces for the burial of the dead went on. Often the fighting was ferocious and destructive, and the slaughter terrible; but little ground was won or lost.

During the periods of truce English, French and Russian officers walked about 'saluting each other courteously and occasionally entering into conversation, and a constant interchange of little civilities, such as offering and receiving cigarlights, was going on in each little group'.

Ironically, while all this civility was going on . . . 'we were walking among the dead; over blood-stained ground, covered with evidences of recent fighting. Broken muskets, bayonets, cartouch-boxes, caps, fragments of clothing, straps and belts, pieces of shell, little pools of clotted blood . . . '

* Immediately after the Battle of the Alma

16

The Sea of Azov is open to us

April/May 1855. Breaks in the deadly monotony of the siege routine were vitally important, to prevent either lethargy or restlessness disrupting the discipline of the ranks. Lord Raglan continued to urge the French to make an all-out attack on Sebastopol, in the hope of bringing the war to an end, but the French generals continually postponed the decisive moment.

Instead, on April 26th, they held a 'grand military spectacle'. The whole of General Bosquet's army, consisting of forty-five battalions of infantry, two regiments of heavy dragoons and two regiments of *Chasseurs d'Afrique*, together with field artillery, was reviewed and inspected by the general, accompanied by a large and 'very brilliant' staff, several English generals and 'an immense field of our officers'.

All told the review lasted almost four hours—right under the noses of the Russians, who did absolutely nothing about it!

A month later a more useful 'spectacular' was planned. Lord Raglan, 'very anxious not to leave the French the credit for doing everything', proposed an allied expedition to destroy the Russian coastal base at Kertch, 150 miles east of Balaklava at the entrance to the Sea of Azov. If successful this would threaten, if not actually cut, the Russian lines of communication and supply from the east.

There was as usual some difference of opinion with the French commanders but finally the expedition set sail: 7,500 French troops, 5,000 Turkish and almost 4,000 British, with a supporting force of warships.

The most strenuous, but luckily unsuccessful, efforts were made by the generals to prevent Russell accompanying the expedition. He wrote to Delane:

⊙ The Expedition starts tomorrow. I have just heard that little Gordon swears he will not let me go, if he searches every ship in the expedition himself . . . He certainly can stop me if he comes across me, so I must try to avoid him . . . ⊙

Large as he was, Russell evidently managed to secrete himself on board the transport *Hope*. The generals were to regret bitterly that they did not search more thoroughly.

As so often in this puzzling war, the allies, once they had decided to take action, swept all before them. They left Balaklava on May 23rd to make the journey of 150 miles, and by May 26th Russell was able to report:

⊙ The success of the expedition by land and sea is complete, rapid and glorious. The forts which defended the narrow and difficult Straits of Kertch have been forced after a feeble resistance, the magazines of the enemy have been exploded by their own hands, all their guns have fallen into our possession, together with a prodigious quantity of corn, grain, munitions of war, naval stores, and military equipment.

The Sea of Azov is open to us, and our flying squadron of steam gunboats is searching it from end to end, burning and destroying the ships and trading vessels of the Russians, crushing their forts and carrying terror and dismay along the seaboard of their inland lake. ⊙

Unfortunately 'ships, trading vessels and forts' were not all that the allied troops were destroying. The 'success and glory' of the exercise was soon swamped by incidents it shamed Russell to record.

May 1855. To his fury and frustration *The Times*'s Correspondent, whose presence could not for long be concealed, was forbidden to land at Yenikale, an important town (which was surrendered to the allies 'without a blow') on the northern bank of the Straits of Kertch, five and a half miles north-east of the town of Kertch itself. On May 25th he wrote privately to Delane:

⊙ As I was going on shore to take up my quarters with the troops, I received a message from Dr Alexander to the effect that Sir George Brown (who commanded the British contingent) swore by G—— that if I ventured to set foot on the beach he would put me in irons.

I have written to ask permission to go on shore but have not yet received his reply. The old brute is quite capable of carrying out his threat, and though I would not care a farthing about the escapade it would expose me to so much ridicule and chaffing that I could not remain with the army; and it would degrade and lower me in the eyes of everyone, and gratify my many enemies . . . ⊙

Sir George's response to Russell's mild request was a brusque refusal. As he told Delane he would, Russell obeyed the command, and did not go ashore at Yenikale . . . but apparently nothing specific was said about his landing, or not landing, at Kertch and, learning by experience, Russell appears to have been wise enough not to ask permission. In fact he never admitted to Sir George that he did go ashore— but private letters written to his chief, plus his dispatch dated May 28th, leave little doubt.

Perhaps because he realised it would raise a storm he began the dispatch defensively . . .

⊙ Before I proceed to narrate the events which have occurred since my last letter . . . I must be permitted to express the sentiments of abhorrence which every civilized being must experience on surveying the scenes of destruction and barbarous violence presented by this unfortunate town, and to protest against any imputation on account of the sacking of Kertch being attached to Englishmen or to any British subject, with the exception of the Lieutenant-General, whose apathy or neglect permitted the perpetration of disgraceful excesses.

When the Russian army, numbering some 2,500 men, abandoned Kertch on the afternoon of our landing at Ambalaki*, a large caravan of the inhabitants, with such property as they could collect in their trepidation, moved out after the soldiery . . . leaving behind their houses full of furniture, and such cumbrous articles as they were unable to move.

When the allies entered Kertch the following morning, the population (left behind) made their submission, and offered bread and salt to the conquerors, in accordance with the Russian custom, and they were assured that they would be protected, and that their lives and property should be spared.

The troops marched on to Yenikale, leaving behind them a few sailors and soldiers to guard Kertch, and to destroy the Government manufactories and a private establishment for making Minié balls and cartridges.

In the afternoon . . . the crews of some merchant ships from Ambalaki landed, and began to break into three or four houses, which had been closed and fastened up, and to pillage the contents. As they could not remove the heavy furniture they smashed it to atoms.

Towards evening Turkish stragglers from the camp, and others who had fallen out of the line of march, flocked into the town, and perpetrated the most atrocious crimes.

To pillage and wanton devastation they added violation and murder. The Tartars who were in the town hailed the arrival of the Osmanli with delight, and received them as

* A small village not far from Kertch and Yenikale—the allies' first landing place

liberators, and as brethren to whom they were bound by the ties of religion, of language, and of hatred to the Russians. They led the few Turks from house to house, pointed out, as victims to their cupidity and lust, those who had made themselves obnoxious to their ignorance or fanaticism, and gratified their ancient grudges to the Russian tradespeople and merchants.

The French patrols endeavoured to preserve order, and succeeded to some extent, but not till they had killed and wounded several Turks and Tartars.

One miscreant was shot as he came down the street in triumph waving a sword wet with the blood of a poor child whom he had hacked to pieces. Others were slain in the very act of committing horrible outrages. Some were borne off wounded to the prison or hospital, and at last respect for life was established by its destruction.

There was not, to be sure, a general massacre. Even savages would have refrained from slaughtering the inhabitants of a town which had submitted, and thrown itself upon their mercy. It was with difficulty, however, that the French controlled the excesses of the Turks, and of some of their own countrymen. ◉

The next day some English merchantmen joined in the pillage and destruction. One of their targets—an act of vandalism which greatly angered Russell—was an ancient temple used as a museum. Its contents, many of them priceless and irreplaceable, were smashed far beyond recovery and repair.

Russell went to see the havoc.

◉ It is impossible to convey an idea of the scene. . . . One might well wonder how the fury of a few men could effect such a prodigious amount of ruin in so short a time.

The floor . . . is covered for several inches in depth with the debris of broken glass, of vases, urns, statuary, the precious dust of their contents and charred bits of wood and bone, mingled with the fresh splinters of the shelves, desks and cases in which they had been preserved.

Not a single bit of anything that could be broken or burnt any smaller had been exempt from reduction by hammer or fire . . .

A large dog lay crouching in fear among the remnants of the vases, and howled dismally at the footsteps of a stranger . . .

One sentry placed at the door would have prevented all this discreditable outrage, which will, no doubt, be attributed by the enemy to our Generals and our troops. For all I know the Tartars may have joined in the destruction of the museum, or the Turks may have been its sole authors; but the blame will, no doubt, be attached to the civilized states whose officers and soldiers took the most active part in the operations against the enemy. ◉

The local Governor's house received similar treatment, and among the articles destroyed here were documents and State papers which could have been not only historically interesting, but perhaps also useful to the allies.

◉ The amount of curious documents and papers in the house of the Chief of Staff was astonishing, and the order and method with which they had been arranged, and the neatness with which they were kept, showed the exactness and carefulness of the Russian government. The registry of vessels entering or passing by Kertch was exceedingly minute and copious, and the notes against some of them was a proof of the surveillance exercised, in peace as in war, by Russia on all her neighbours.

What a pity that these documents should be destroyed! Many a strange dark secret may lie buried with them for ever. ◉

Russell goes on to list the more legitimate plunder— military and naval stores (including 'an infernal machine of curious construction') either annexed or destroyed by the allies.

By the time they had finished there was virtually nothing left of the town, either as a place to live, or as a military strongpoint.

Although he had been refused permission to land at Yenikale, and might therefore have taken some sort of literary revenge on the British Commander, in fact Russell tried to minimise (though without much show of conviction) the responsibility for the wholesale destruction both here and at Ambalaki which might otherwise automatically have fallen on Sir George's head.

⊙ It will be remembered that our troops marched through Kertch on Friday, the 25th May, and occupied Yenikale early on the same day. The same attempts to destroy the property of the people of Yenikale which were so successful at Kertch were made by the troops, but they were repressed by the Generals, and Sir George Brown took some steps to prevent the dilapidation of the houses by the French, under the pretence that they required fuel.

Nevertheless, nearly every house in the town was broken into and plundered, and the furniture was smashed to pieces. Several buildings were set on fire, and were with difficulty extinguished, and at one time the greater part of the houses were threatened with destruction, as the wind blew the flames in the direction of the principal street. ⊙

This, and very much more, Russell poured out in white-hot indignation, adding:

⊙ It is very unpleasant to have to darken the picture of our success with a dash of the same gloomy old colour which rose out of the Balaklava mud, but justice must be done, and truth must be told . . . ⊙

Sir George, of course, was livid. Later he taxed Russell with making him appear to the world 'as a barbarian'.

'You should have known that I was in no way responsible for what happened at Kertch, any more than you were,' he added angrily.

179

'But how could I know *who* was responsible?' Russell replied blandly. 'You forbade me to go ashore to see *for myself* what was happening, didn't you?'

Sir George was silenced. Either he must accuse Russell of telling lies, or basing his reports on hearsay; or accept the fact that his explicit orders had been defied. The first alternative was dangerous, the second unpalatable.

Sir George withdrew from the field, leaving Russell, for once, victorious.

17
They lay where they fell
(The first attack on the Redan)

June 1855. Russell returned from Kertch to find W. H. Stowe, his temporary replacement in the field, dying of cholera in his hut. Because he was a civilian Stowe had been refused admission to the military hospital, in spite of the fact that his official position was that of administrator of the famous *Times* Fund raised expressly to provide stocks of medical supplies, when Florence Nightingale set out for the Crimea!

Russell at once used his influence to have him moved to Balaklava, where he could receive proper attention. But it was too late. Stowe lived only a very short time longer.

The Times, not unnaturally, was not slow to mention this 'martyrdom', adding that it would not risk another life to a service in which, among other dangers, 'British inhumanity is to be encountered'.

Meanwhile, plans were going ahead for a heavy bombardment of Sebastopol, prior to an all-out assault. (Even the

French Generals by now realised that this could not be postponed much longer.) But for the moment 'the fighting was done by jerks and starts, and the combatants, like Homer's heroes, stood at ease the best part of the time and took it coolly . . . '

On June 7th rumours began to fly—something was going to happen, at last.

In fact the plan was for a French assault on the Mamelon— the fortified hill-position in front of the Malakoff fortress, towards which the Russian trenches had been creeping for months.

While this was going on the British were to distract the Russians' attention by attacking the Quarries, another defensive position in front of the Redan fortress.

⊙ It was about half-past six (in the evening) when the head of the French attacking column came into view . . . as it climbed its arduous road to the Mamelon.

A rocket was instantly thrown up as the signal for our diversion, and as instantly the small force of our men detached for the post of honour made a rush at the Quarries.

After one slight check they drove out the Russians, and, turning round the gabions, commenced making themselves snug; but interest was so entirely concentrated upon the more exciting scene, full in view upon the right, that they had to wait a good while before attention was directed to their conflict.

The French went up the steep to the Mamelon in most beautiful style and in loose order, and every straining eye was upon their movements, which the declining daylight did not throw out into bold relief.

Still their figures, like light shadows flitting across the dun barrier of earthworks, were seen to mount up unfailingly, running, climbing, scrambling like skirmishers up the slopes on to the body of the work, amid a plunging fire from the

181

guns which, owing to their loose formation, did them as yet little damage.

As an officer who saw Bosquet wave them on, said at the moment, 'They went in like a clever pack of hounds.'

In a moment some of these dim wraiths shone out clear against the sky. The Zouaves were upon the parapet firing down into the place from above; the next moment a flag was up as a rallying-point and defiance, and was seen to sway hither and thither, now up, now down, as the tide of battle raged about it; and now like a swarm they were in the heart of the Mamelon and a fierce hand-to-hand encounter, here with the musket, there with the bayonet, was evident. ◉

It all happened incredibly quickly. The French were inside the fortification eight minutes from the start of the assault. But it was not over yet. The Russians fought like tigers and at times it was difficult to see who was 'on top'.

◉ It was growing dark, and difficult to distinguish one army from the other. At one moment it seemed that the French were over-running the Mamelon, at the next that the Russians were driving them back . . . but at last, and with swelling excitement . . . through the twilight, we discerned that the French were pouring in . . . the swell and babble of the fight was once more rolling down the inner face of the hill . . . the Russians were conclusively beaten. ◉

Intoxicated by their success—the first really decisive success in battle the allies had won since the Alma—the French troops swept on towards the Malakoff Tower, part of the main fortifications of Sebastopol.

◉ The Tower itself, or rather the inglorious stump of what was once the Tower, took and gave shot and shell and musketry with the most savage ardour and rapidity.

The fire of its musketry was like one sheet of flame, rolling backwards and forwards with a dancing movement, and, dwarfed as it was by the distance and seen by us in profile, could scarcely be compared to anything except the notes of a piano flashed into fire throughout some rapid tune.

Our gunners . . . pitched their shells into the tower with admirable precision, doing immense mischief to the defenders. The Russian defence, rather than their defences, crumbled away before this tremendous fire . . . ⊙

But the attack on the Malakoff not having been planned, there was no backing-up of the first impulsive dash and the attempt 'languished, and gradually died away'.

During the night the Russians tried desperately to drive the British troops from the Quarries, and to restore the damage to their more important defence works. The two armies were so close together that 'the sentinels outside our advanced works could hear the sound of their tools, and see the light of their tobacco pipes'.

On the morning of June 9th the Russians petitioned for and were granted a truce for the removal and burial of the dead, and 'from one o'clock until six in the evening no shot was fired on either side'.

The truth was that, although Lord Raglan and his senior officers were anxious to press ahead with a combined assault on the two great fortifications of the Malakoff and Redan Towers, once again French caution held the allied armies back. With some justification they believed that the Russian fire-power was too great; that the allies must build up their own batteries to overcome this before making a frontal attack.

The days dragged by. June 18th was set for the assault. Again Lord Raglan was not entirely happy about the tactical details worked out by the French Generals, but as always he accepted their judgement.

The general idea was that the allies should press forward from the positions they had captured early in the month; the French to attack the Malakoff Tower and the British the Redan.

On Sunday the 17th a heavy bombardment was carried

out, and then early on Monday morning the troops moved
down the trenches.

For the last remaining hours of darkness they waited in
mounting tension. There was silence and darkness all along
the front, broken only by the occasional roar and blinding
flash of a bomb.

⊚ Just as some faint tinge of light in the east announced
the approach of dawn, we heard a very irregular but sharp
fire of musketry on our right, close to the Malakoff.

In an instant all the Russian works on the right woke up
into life, and the roar of artillery, mingled with musketry,
became incessant . . . ⊚

It was to be a typically Crimean war day of mistakes and
misunderstandings: signals misinterpreted, not received, or
never made at all; too few men, or men in the wrong places.

The Russians, too, proved for once to have outwitted the
allies by masking their guns or withdrawing them from the
embrasures as if they were overpowered and silenced by
allied fire—so that the great weight of their bombardment
took the French and British troops by surprise.

The whole affair was a dismal failure.

⊚ . . . In no case did the troops destined to assault and
carry the Redan reach the outer part of the work . . . no
ladders were placed in the ditch, and a very small portion
indeed of the storming party reached the abattis, which was
placed many yards in front of the ditch of the Redan.

It cannot be said that on this occasion our men exhibited
any want of courage; but so abortive and so weak was the
attack, that the Russians actually got outside the parapet of
the Redan, jeered and laughed at our soldiers as they fired
upon them at the abattis, and mockingly invited the 'In-
glisky' to come nearer . . . ⊚

Now it was the allies' turn to sue for a truce so that they
could bury their dead and carry their wounded from the

field. The petition was made early in the day but for some inscrutable reason it was arranged that the armistice should not begin until four o'clock in the afternoon.

Meanwhile the sun mounted in the sky and the heat grew intense.

⊙ It was agonizing to see the wounded men who were lying there under a broiling sun, parched with excruciating thirst, racked with fever, and agonized with pain—to behold them waving their caps faintly or making signals towards our lines, over which they could see the white flag waving . . .

They lay where they fell, or had scrambled into the holes formed by the shells; and there they had been for thirty hours. An officer told me that one soldier who was close to the abattis, when he saw a few men come out of an embrasure, raised himself on his elbow, and fearing he should be unnoticed and passed by, raised his cap on a stick and waved it till he fell back exhausted.

Again he rose, and managed to tear off his shirt, which he agitated in the air till his strength failed him. His face could be seen through a glass; and my friend said he never could forget the expression of resignation and despair with which the poor fellow at last folded his shirt under his head to await the mercy of Heaven. ⊙

Russell rode with some friends out on to the battlefield where 'the red-coats lay sadly thick over the broken ground' and into the Mamelon where 'the interior was like a quarry, so torn and blown up with shells'.

⊙ The stench was fearful. It arose from the dead Russians, who had been buried as they fell, and bones and arms and legs stuck out from the piles of rubbish on which you were treading.

Many guns were also buried here when they had been disabled by our fire . . . ⊙

Movement round about the fortification was made hazardous by a primitive but dangerous sort of mine which exploded

185

at the touch of a foot. Russell was only just prevented from blowing himself to smithereens on one of these contraptions by an alert and 'kindly' British sentry.

The time for the truce came at last and:

⊙ The bodies of many a brave officer whom I had known in old times—old times of the war, for men's lives were short in the Crimea, and the events of a life were compressed into a few hours—were borne past us in silence; and now and then, wonderful to relate, men with severe wounds were found still living and able to give expression to their sufferings by moans and sighs of pain. ⊙

Russian sentries patrolled during the removal and burial of the dead and Russell noticed the difference between their appearance, and that of the allies. They were:

⊙ . . . fine, tall, muscular, and soldier-like fellows, and one could not but contrast them with some of the poor weakly-looking boys who were privates in our regiments, or with the small undergrown men of the French line.

They were unusually well-dressed, in clean new uniforms . . . Many wore medals and seemed veteran soldiers. Their officers . . . wore white kid gloves, patent leather boots, and white linen. ⊙

The armistice lasted for two hours. When it was over the allies retired from 'the spot so moistened with our blood'.

The British had lost more than 1,500 officers and men, killed and wounded, and the French around 1,700. The only material gain was the capture by the British of a small cemetery, five hundred yards from the Redan.

June/July 1855. It was not only amongst the men, and junior officers, that death in battle and through sickness was taking its toll.

Lord Raglan looked 'far from well', and according to Russell had aged greatly. General Estcourt, Adjutant-General of the Army, died from cholera on June 24th after only three days' illness. Early in July Sir George Brown left the Crimea on 'sick certificate'.

Russell heard about General Estcourt's death shortly after he himself had left the front for a well-earned leave at Therapia, on the Bosphorus, having been told that no attempt would be made to renew the assault on Sebastopol for several weeks.

With some reluctance the Manager of *The Times*, Mowbray Morris, had agreed that Mrs Russell should join her husband for a month, though he made it very clear that he regarded this as a great concession. At the expiration of the month, he wrote severely, Mrs Russell was to return to England, and Russell himself to his duties.

⊙ If you were an officer with a wife and young family in England, I should never advise your wife's joining you for any length of time and leaving her children, except in the event of your being seriously wounded; and I cannot see anything in your position which materially distinguishes it from that of an officer.

There is every disposition among us all to alleviate your separation from your family in every reasonable way; but I shall never cease to oppose your wife's permanent residence in Constantinople whilst the duties of your correspondence require you to be with the Army.

I acknowledge that your case is a hard one, but it is not harder than that of thousands of other good fellows, who submit to fate with more or less grace, as you have done and will continue to do . . . ⊙

Almost immediately he had left Balaklava the news reached Russell of the death on June 28th of Lord Raglan. The Commander-in-Chief had never fully recovered from the shock, distress and disappointment of the short inglorious struggle to capture the Redan, on top of all his other anxieties and disappointments. The immediate cause of death was

187

'a fever'—not, according to the doctors, cholera—but the probability is that in the end he simply 'gave up'.

Russell was 'sensibly shocked' at the news. Although he had fiercely attacked Lord Raglan time and again for what he considered sins of omission, as a man Russell liked and admired him. He was, Russell wrote:

◉ . . . an amiable, honourable, kindly man, animated by zeal for the public service, of the most unswerving fidelity to truth, devoted to his duty and to his profession . . . ◉

But all of this did not blind Russell to the fact that he was also:

◉ . . . a man of strong prejudices and weak resolution, possessed of limited information, offensively cold to those whom, like Omar Pasha (the Turkish Commander-in-Chief) he considered vulgar or obtrusive, coerced without difficulty by the influence of a stronger will, and too apt to depend upon those around him when he should have used his own eyes.

Still, there was a simplicity about his manner, something of the old heroic type in his character, which would have compensated for even graver defects, if their results had not been, in many instances, so unfortunate for our arms. ◉

As a soldier he was, Russell wrote:

◉ . . . perhaps an unexceptionable lieutenant under a great chief; but that he was a great chief, or even a moderately able general, I have every reason to doubt, and I look in vain for any proof of it whilst he commanded the English Army in the Crimea. ◉

The argument about Russell's 'defamation' of Lord Raglan —even his part-responsibility for the old General's death— continued to rage after the war was over. He was even accused of statements or comments he had never made. Defending himself in a book about the Crimean campaign, *The Great War with Russia*, he wrote:

◉ Soon after the close of the war the Earl of Dartmouth thought fit . . . to accuse me of using the most offensive language about Lord Raglan in my correspondence. I immediately challenged his lordship to point out a single passage in any of my letters in support of his charge.

The Earl of Dartmouth's reply was disingenuous. He sought to fix on me the responsibility of articles written in London when I was many hundreds of miles away, and of which I knew as little as he did.

'You were the correspondent of *The Times*! *The Times* attacked Lord Raglan! Therefore you attacked Lord Raglan! Q.E.D.!!'

It was a false and scandalous imputation. I was led to look out every passage in which Lord Raglan's name was mentioned in 'Letters from the Crimea' and to submit them to calm and impartial men for their judgement, and I am prepared to do the same today.

Not one sentence, not one line, not one word is there to be found in my letters in which Lord Raglan is mentioned in any way but with the respect that was his due . . .

I set forth with all the force of words of which I was capable the sense I entertained of the nobility of Lord Raglan's character; but I did not shrink from expressing the opinion that he had the faults of his virtues and of the amiable disposition that shunned argument, contention, and stern resolves, and gave way under pressure, and that he was not a great general. ◉

This was by no means the end of the affair. Russell and Lord Dartmouth carried on a correspondence on the subject, on and off, for twenty-one years!

Lieutenant-General James Simpson was appointed Lord Raglan's successor. In spite of the change of Government, and the bitter experiences of more than a year at war, the powers-that-were seemed no more capable of choosing a leader for the army than they had been at the beginning. General Simpson, according to Russell, was:

◉ . . . certainly not suited to resist any pressure which

our allies might think fit to apply; and he was destitute of those acquirements and personal characteristics which in Lord Raglan compensated for a certain apathy and marble calmness which his admirers extolled as virtues . . . ⊙

It was believed by many people at the time that General Simpson had actually opposed his own appointment 'and bore testimony to his own incapacity', but the Government insisted, and the General was 'drafted' to the job as Commander-in-Chief of the British Army.

18
Motionless and expectant

July/August 1855. Russell's holiday lasted a little longer than originally planned, as he was attacked by 'Crimean fever' shortly after his arrival on the Bosphorus. But he did not waste his time. As always, ears and eyes were wide open and busy among the sick and wounded officers recuperating at the Hotel d'Angleterre before returning to the front. They made depressing company.

⊙ . . . There was a great desire among young and old to get away from the Crimea on any pretence, in order to escape for a time from the sanguinary monotony of trench duties, the harassing sounds of cannon and rifle, which beat on the ear day and night, and the contagious influence of gloomy thoughts. ⊙

There was a great deal of discussion about the conduct of the war, and the arrival of news from the Crimea was the one event looked forward to each day.

The general feeling was that with the attack on the Redan the first great phase in the siege had been passed.

⊙ We found that the Russians could resist the allied forces with vigour, and that they were capable of acting upon the defensive with greater energy than we gave them credit for from their conduct at the Alma. ⊙

It was not a cheering thought. To make things worse the generals now in command were new and untried, even by comparison with those who had first led the Crimean campaign; and while cholera still steadily diminished the allied ranks, the Russians were receiving enormous reinforcements.

But it was obvious that there was no thought yet of giving up. The constant passage up the Bosphorus of ships with troops from France, and artillery and other material from England 'evinced the preparations made by the allies for the renewal of the struggle'.

The idea met with little enthusiasm among the sick and wounded officers at Therapia. There were many who thought that the siege would—at best—not be over till the following year, and that they would have to endure the miseries of a second winter in the open trenches.

Back at the front Russell found himself assailed by the usual myriad irritations and inconveniences which were almost more trying than the dangers and strains of war . . . and was reminded that summer could be quite as uncomfortable a season in the Crimea as winter had been.

⊙ Every nook and cranny was infested with millions of flies, which gave one no rest by day and little by night.

Situated as I was in the delightful vicinity of several hundred commissariat mules, and a varied assortment of empty sugar barrels and receptacles for beef and pork, it was possible I might have had more than my share of the attentions of these pertinacious insects, which hovered on every side in clouds and settled on the most irritable parts of the face without giving a moment's relaxation.

Like the Harpies, they literally 'disputed the viands', such as they were, on which we regaled ourselves, a morsel in its passage to the mouth being generally settled upon by two or more of the insects, which required a vigorous shaking before they would let go their hold. ◉

The French had now extended their trenches forward from the Mamelon (the fortified hill-position they captured early in June) almost as far as the Malakoff fortress; so near, in fact, that as Russell said 'a man might throw a stone into the Russian position'. He went on:

◉ The surface of the ground in the neighbourhood of the Malakoff and the Redan presented every day a more checkered appearance. It was one mass of trenches, traverses, rifle-pits, and batteries—a perfect maze, so that it required a strongly developed organ of locality, or else many days' practise of trench duties, to enable one to find one's way. ◉

But, though rumours flew, nothing very much happened, apart from the occasional sortie. The twin Crimean evils, boredom and sickness, hung over the summer-heavy land. Russell found time to grumble again about the Turks, who 'never took part in the siege'.

◉ It is a singular thing [he remarked aggrievedly] that while the French and British troops consider their most harassing work to be the duty of the trenches, the Turks, who are equally interested in the event of the war, and will be the most benefited by its success, do not take any share in actual siege operations and amuse themselves with the mere past-time of foraging, or actually sitting in indolence for hours together, following the shadows of their tents as they move from west to east, smoking stolidly, or grinning at the antics of some mountebank comrade . . . ◉

He had a slightly more unusual incident to report early in August.

◉ Three nights ago a buxom *cantinière* accompanied her battalion to the trenches, there to supply them with the restorative *petit verre*, and to brave, with masculine courage, the storm of shot and shell.

192

There was possibly some miscalculation in the matter; but the fact is that, towards the small hours of the morning, she was taken with the pains of maternity, and gave birth to twins.

Mother and children are doing well . . . ⊙

The most frequent rumour, as the summer began to run downhill, was of an approaching attack on the Malakoff fortress. General Simpson was observed making the rounds of the lines and examining the works. He was closely followed by General Sir Harry Jones, Chief Officer of the Royal Engineers.

Orders were received to clear the hospitals and send to Balaklava such patients as could safely be moved, and to make preparation for the reception of wounded men. Something was obviously afoot.

Strategy and tactics were knowledgeably discussed over the rum rations in a dozen different tents, by junior officers as well as generals.

Then, at last:

⊙ Late in the evening [of the 12th August] orders were given for the troops to be under arms by three in the morning. Of course, Malakoff was immediately the word, and most persons supposed that the long-talked-of assault was to be made. This, however, was soon found not to be the case. An attack was expected to take place along the whole line. ⊙

There was little sleep for anyone. These might, after all, be the last few hours of stagnation—the last night before the action which was to end the long agony of the Crimea.

Men lay, talking quietly, smoking their pipes, staring into the darkness. Waiting. . . . Outside the tents horses stamped and snorted, catching the mood of half-fearful anticipation. After midnight the tension grew. Figures began to flit quietly about. There was the subdued jingle of harness.

⊙ Without tap of drum or sound of bugle, the camp was afoot . . . the troops forming up in profound silence. The entire army was out, including the cavalry and artillery from Balaklava.

The first grey of morning found a number of officers and 'amateurs' assembled on Cathcart's Hill, the best point of observation . . . as the morning advanced . . . the scarlet columns became visible, massed along the lines motionless and expectant.

Superior officers, with their staff, moved to and fro; aides-de-camp traversed the heights with orders; here and there, through the still imperfect light which began to be tinged with the first red flush of sunrise, waved the pennons of a Lancer escort . . . ◉

It was a moment of almost unbearable strain. And, as so often, it ended on a note of anti-climax.

◉ Before the upper edge of the sun's disc rose above the hills, the troops were marching briskly back to their tents. In serried columns, looking hardy, active and cheerful, and up to any work, the Crimean army regained its canvas quarters. For the day, the danger was over—to commence again, it was believed, at night. . . . The officers were warned to be ready at a moment's notice. ◉

Why was there no action? Russell reports that General Simpson was 'indisposed' and proposed withdrawing to one of the ships in Balaklava harbour for a few days, and that he had summoned his subordinates to a conference before doing so. It seems a curious moment to have chosen.

An alternative explanation, incredibly, was that the assembly of the troops was a mere 'rehearsal'.

One thing seems certain—large numbers of reinforcements had arrived in Sebastopol, and had been seen collecting behind the Redan . . .

19

About daybreak the cannonade began . . .
(The Battle of the Tchernaya)

August 1855. In the end it was not the allies who initiated the fighting, but the Russians.

The attack came from the north-east, across the River Tchernaya—the last of the rivers the allies had had to cross on their flank-march from Eupatoria to Balaklava in the early days of the campaign. It caught them a sideways blow at one of the weakest places on the front, but it can hardly have been said to be entirely unexpected.

⊙ Several deserters came on the 15th [August] and spoke with the utmost certainty of an intended attack on the Tchernaya; but no particular attention was paid to their reports, and no special orders were given to the troops, except to be prepared. No additional precautions were taken on the Tchernaya line and the advance was scarcely less a surprise than that of Inkerman. ⊙

The first shock was taken by the French and the 15,000 Sardinian troops who had come out in May. The British were not involved in this action.

⊙ The first news of an actual assault was brought about daybreak by some French Chasseurs, who, forming part of a patrol, fell into an ambuscade of the Russians and narrowly escaped, while their comrades were taken prisoners.

Soon afterwards the outposts across the Tchernaya were driven in, and about daybreak the cannonade began . . . ⊙

Meanwhile, unconscious that fighting had already begun, the French Light Infantry in forward posts were just beginning to rub the sleep from their eyes. *Réveillé* had not yet

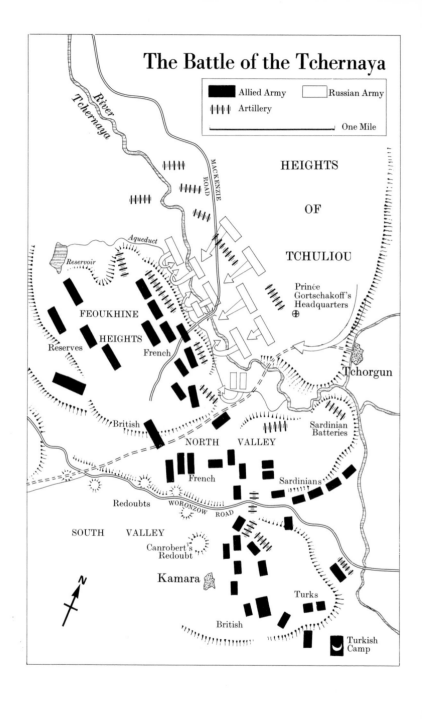

The Battle of the Tchernaya

Allied Army   Russian Army

Artillery

One Mile

River Tchernaya

MACKENZIE ROAD

HEIGHTS

OF

TCHULIOU

Aqueduct

Reservoir

FEOUKHINE

HEIGHTS

Reserves

French

Prince Gortschakoff's Headquarters

Tchorgun

British

NORTH VALLEY

Sardinian Batteries

French

Sardinians

Redoubts

WORONZOW ROAD

SOUTH VALLEY

Canrobert's Redoubt

Kamara

Turks

British

Turkish Camp

N

officially sounded.

⊙ . . . but some of the men were already busy preparing
their coffee, when the sentinels in advance were alarmed by
hearing close at hand the tramp of men, whose forms were
yet invisible in the darkness.

Discharging their muskets, they ran in to the posts, who
had not time to stand to their arms ere they were engaged
with overwhelming masses of the enemy.

They were driven across the river; but the desultory firing
which took place in this preliminary skirmish had given
timely warning to the main guards and to the camps, and the
men turned out just as a storm of round shot began to rush
over the ground, upsetting camp-kettles, dashing out fires,
and destroying tents in its career. ⊙

Despite the advantage of 'surprise', the Russians failed to
carry through that first attack, and the allies had an ill-
deserved second chance to pull themselves together.

For once Russell himself was late on the scene. The battle
had been raging for an hour before he reached the line of the
French works.

⊙ From the high grounds over which I had to ride, the
whole of the battle-field was marked out by rolling columns
of smoke and irregular thick puffs of the artillery.

All our cavalry camps were deserted; but the sun played
on the helmets and sabres of the solid squadrons which were
drawn up about two miles in advance of Kadikoi, and just in
rear of the line of hills which the French and Sardinians were
defending, so as to be ready to charge the Russians, should
they force the position. ⊙

At last, a little late, the allies were ready—and the Russians never really regained the initiative. They crossed the
river in force in a number of places and began to scale the
heights beyond, but the French and Sardinians stood fast.

It was a gallant and determined attack . . .

⊙ On they came, as it seemed, irresistible, and rushed up

A Zouave sentry, watching the Russians encamped at Tchernaya

the steep hill with such fury that the Zouaves, who lined the sides of it, were obliged to fall back for a moment before the multitude.

The officers might be seen leading the way and animating their soldiers. One gallant fellow, at least twenty yards in advance of the whole column, was the first to cross the aqueduct* and was afterwards seen on the side of the hill. ◉

But the French had not been idle during the time that the Russians were ascending the hill. The Zouaves had only fallen back from the side of the hillock to the main body, which had been drawn up behind the top.

◉ Scarcely did the column of the enemy show its head, when the guns opened upon it with grape, and a murderous fire was poured among its ranks by the French infantry.

* An artificial 'waterway' on the allied side of the river which ran parallel to it for some distance. Nine or ten feet wide and several feet deep, it formed the chief defence of the French

This immediately stopped the advance of the column, which began to waver; but the impetus from those behind was so powerful that the head of it notwithstanding the unexpected reception, was pushed forward a few yards more, when the French, giving one mighty cheer, rushed upon the advancing enemy, who, shaken already, immediately turned round and ran down, if possible, faster than they had come up . . . ◉

So sudden and complete was the reverse that the Russians blocked their own retreat. More than two hundred prisoners, unable to fight their way back through the ranks of their own comrades, were taken; while the hillside, the river-side and all the surrounding areas were filled with dead and wounded.

◉ The Sardinian and French artillery poured, moreover, a murderous cross-fire into the scattered remains of the column, and scarcely a shot missed. It was a complete rout. ◉

It was not the end of the engagement. The Russians bravely collected the scattered remnants of their army along other sections of the front, made one more crossing of the river and began to storm the heights.

◉ . . . but in vain; the French were now thoroughly prepared, and the tenacity of the Russians only served to augment their losses. They were soon seen fleeing in all directions, followed by the French . . . ◉

It was the end of the Battle of the Tchernaya. A defiant crackle of rifle fire from the Russian side of the river did little damage, and a battalion of Piedmontese, preceded by a company of Bersaglierie 'advanced in beautiful order as if on parade, and soon drove these riflemen from their position'.

By ten o'clock 'the dust on the Mackenzie Road and the black lines moving off were the only traces which remained of the so long threatened attack of the Russians'.

◉ Everybody now rushed to the battlefield, and one look

was sufficient to convince them that the Allies had won a real battle. Although not quite so obstinate and sanguinary as the battle of Inkerman, which this affair resembled in many points, it was a pitched battle.

The Russians, as in the battle of Inkerman, gave up manœuvring, and confided entirely in the valour of their troops. The essential difference was in the manner of fighting. At the Inkerman the great mass of the Russians fell under the file firing and the bayonets of the infantry, while on the Tchernaya it was the guns which did the greatest execution.

Most of the wounded and dead showed frightful traces of round-shot, grape, shell, and canister, so that, as a battle-field, one could scarcely imagine anything more terrible. Nearly all the wounds were on the legs and the head.

On the banks of the aqueduct particularly, the sight was appalling; the Russians, when scaling the embankment of the aqueduct, were taken in flank by the Sardinian batteries, and the dead and wounded rolled down the embankment, some-times more than twenty feet . . . ⊙

Leaving their dead behind, the defeated army of the Czar began its long retreat.

⊙ The march of the Russians continued till late in the day —their last column gained the plateau about two o'clock. It must have been a terrible march for them—not a drop of water to be had; and even when they gained their arid camp (on the heights to the east of Sebastopol) it is only too prob-able that they had nothing to drink; indeed, the prisoners told us the men were encouraged to the attack by being told that if they gained the Tchernaya they would have abun-dance of water—the greatest inducement that could be held out to them. ⊙

There was one last burst of defiance.

⊙ I rode down towards the *tête du pont*. In order to get a good view of the retreat I descended to the bridge, which was covered with wounded men. Just as I gained the centre of it, a volley of shells was pitched right upon it, amid the French who, with their usual humanity, were helping the wounded.

Some burst in the shallow stream, the sides of which were crowded with wounded men; others killed poor wretches who were crawling towards the water—one in particular to whom I had just an instant before thrown a sandwich; others knocked pieces out of the bridge or tore up the causeway.

As the road was right in the line of fire, I at once turned off the bridge and, pulling sharp round, dashed under an arch just as the battery opened on us a second time, and there I remained for about ten minutes, when the Russians gave us a respite for a few moments.

The next time they fired was with round shot; and as I retreated up the road to obtain shelter behind one of the hills, one of these knocked a wounded Zouave to pieces before my eyes.

In the rear of the hill there was a party of about five hundred Russian prisoners encamped. Many of them were wounded; all were war-worn, dirty, ill-clad—some in rags, others almost bootless.

The French sentries who guarded them seemed to commiserate with the poor fellows; but two or three of their own officers, who sat apart, did not look at them, but smoked their cigars with great nonchalance, or talked glibly to the French officers of the fortune of war, etc.

In a short time I returned to the front, and saw General Simpson and a few staff officers descending from the Sardinian position, whence they had watched the battle.

The aspect of the field, of the aqueduct, and of the river, was horrible beyond description; the bodies were closely packed in parties, and lay in files two and three deep, where the grape had torn through the columns.

For two days the bodies rotted on the ground which lay beyond the French lines, and the first Russian burying party did not come down till the 18th, when the stench was so very

201

great that the men could scarcely perform their loathsome task. ◉

The scavengers were soon out after Tchernaya, and 'those curiosity-seeking persons whose name was legion, in the allied armies'.

◉ Officers and soldiers, although numerous enough, were few in proportion to the merchants, sailors, suttlers (provision merchants) from Balaklava and Kamiesch, and other nondescript camp-followers, who formed a class of themselves, and were as sure to appear after an action was over as vultures.

They had little chance of getting hold of medals, amulets, and crosses, and other more valuable spoil, for these disappeared marvellously; but they were not particular. The greatest mania seemed to prevail for muskets—nevertheless, cartridge-boxes, swords, bayonets etc. were taken for want of something better. ◉

Short as the encounter on the banks of the Tchernaya had been, the maiming and slaughter was appalling, especially among the Russians.

◉ . . . after a time it was officially known that the French had 2,200 Russian wounded and prisoners, the number of unwounded prisoners amounting to 400.

The collecting of the wounded took nearly two days and most likely there are still some of them not discovered, among the bushes in the neighbourhood of the river . . .

For the burial of the dead an armistice was concluded, during which the French buried all those upon our side of the river, while the Russians buried those in the plain beyond.

Of course the number of those buried by the Russians can never be ascertained, but their number must have been prodigious, for large spaces were cleared in the dense columns by grape and shell; besides the Russians fired with grape into their own people from behind. I heard so from many people, and saw it myself . . . ⊙

After the battlefield had been cleared the French and Sardinian troops set about repairing and strengthening their defences. The Turks had more 'important' things on their minds. It was time for their religious festival Korban Bairam. There was, Russell reported, 'no end to sweetmeats and visiting'.

He went on:

⊙ The solemnity of the occasion seemed to have acted powerfully on their religious feelings; for in passing through their camp at the hours of prayer whole battalions might be seen going through their prayers and protestations. Each battalion had a space cleared for the purpose, and it was provided with the few arrangements which their simple worship required.

Some . . . had only a stick planted in a south-easterly direction; others . . . made enclosures of earth or wickerwork pulpits and in one place even a minaret was erected in a most primitive way—it consisted of nothing but slender poles interwoven with branches of brushwood.

By coming into contact with Europeans the Turks did not seem to have lost any of their zeal for their religion; although no one was forced to take part in the prayers, there were but few absentees from service, particularly in the evening. ⊙

The British had their own way of passing the time and keeping up their spirits between skirmishes, bombardments, and the endless repairs to defences. Sailors from ships in Balaklava Bay were among the most enterprising morale-boosters:

⊙ THEATRE ROYAL, NAVAL BRIGADE
On Friday evening, 31st of August, will be performed
DEAF AS A POST!
To be followed by
THE SILENT WOMAN
The whole to conclude with the laughable Farce entitled

SLASHER AND CRASHER

Seats to be taken at 7 o'clock. Performance to commence
precisely at 8 o'clock

God Save the Queen!   Rule Britannia!

And right well they played [Russell commented after-wards]. True the theatre was the amputating house of the Brigade, but no reflections as to its future and past use marred the sense of present enjoyment.

The scenes were furnished from 'The London',* the actors from the Brigade. There was an agreeable ballet girl, who had to go into the trenches to work a 68-pounder at three o'clock in the morning, and Rosa was impersonated by a pre-possessing young boatswain's mate.

Songs there were in plenty, with a slight smack of the forecastle; but they were all highly appreciated, and the dancing was pronounced to be worthy of Her Majesty's [Theatre] . . .

The sense of enjoyment was not marred by the long range guns, which now and then sent lobbing shot near the theatre and never did any harm; and if the audience were amused, so were the performers, who acted with surprising spirit and taste. ◉

There was, however, a good deal of sickness, which caused Russell no surprise, for 'the recruits sent out to us are miser-able. When in full dress they are "all helmets and boots".'

Men were still being lost in large numbers by enemy action, too, even though there were no large-scale formal attacks by either side. According to the French Commander-in-Chief, he 'lost a fine brigade every ten days'.

It was no compensation, Russell wrote, that 'the enemy loses three to our one. The Russians swarm like flies, and their Generals are only puzzled how to use them, or they could have twice as many.'

* One of the ships in Balaklava harbour

Some of these swarming Russians deserted, though, bringing useful information with them.

⊙ . . . [two] daring fellows in their fear actually swam out last night to one of the French ships on guard off Sebastopol and gave information of great importance.

They declared that most of the heavy guns have been transferred from Fort Constantine and Fort Nicholas to the defensive works, and that the powder is removed from the works of the harbour and placed in Fort Nicholas.

The number of men who started on this perilous expedition was five, and as only two arrived safely, the rest are supposed to have perished. They supported themselves during their long swim by means of bladders . . . ⊙

The allies buoyed themselves up with tenuous hopes, and rumours of peace.

⊙ We had a peace party in camp, who reasoned that the Russians could sustain the contest no longer, owing to the want of water and the difficulty of obtaining supplies . . .

According to these authorities, in a couple of months the British army was to go home again. The hopefulness of youth, and a certain vivacity of imagination, doubtless qualify a man to produce rose-tinted sketches of this kind, and there certainly could be no manner of question as to the immense superiority of a merry Christmas in England to a muddy one on the heights of Balaklava . . .

But there is no magic in wishes any more than in words and these prophets of peace under-rated the tenacity and endurance of the Russian government and people . . . ⊙

20

The Malakoff is safe
(The second attack on the Redan)

September 1855. Finally it was the allies who broke the endless-seeming deadlock, after waiting with fading hopes for the Russians to venture out of their safe fortress and face the entrenched opposition, now ready and waiting for them on the open plain.

On September 5th the batteries opened fire for the sixth time on Sebastopol.

⊙ The air was pure and light, and a gentle breeze from the south-west which continued all day, drifted over the steppe and blew gently into Sebastopol. The sun shone serenely through the vapours of early morning and wreaths of snowy clouds, on the long lines of white houses inside those rugged defences . . . which have so long kept our armies gazing in vain on this august city.

The ships floated quietly on the waters of the roads, which were smooth as a mirror . . . while outside our own fleet and that of the French were reposing . . . as idly as though they were 'painted ships upon a painted ocean'.

Suddenly, close to the Bastion du Mât three jets of flame sprang up into the air and hurled up as many pillars of earth and dust, a hundred feet high, which was warmed into ruddy hues by the horizontal rays of the sun.

The French had exploded three fougasses to blow in the counterscarp and serve as a signal to their men.

In a moment, from the sea to the Dockyard creek, a stream of fire three miles in length seemed to run like a train from battery to battery, and fleecy, curling, rich white smoke

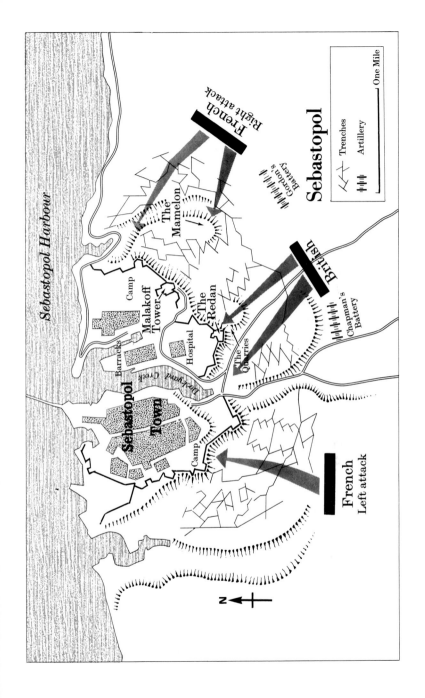

Sebastopol Harbour

Sebastopol Town

Dockyard Creek

Barracks

Camp

Malakoff Tower

Hospital

The Redan

The Quarries

Camp

The Mamelon

Chapman's Battery

Gordon's Battery

Sebastopol

French
Right attack

British

French
Left attack

Trenches
Artillery

One Mile

N

ascended, as though the earth had suddenly been rent in the throes of an earthquake and was vomiting forth the material of her volcanoes.

The lines of the French trenches were at once covered as though the very clouds of Heaven had settled down upon them and were whirled about in spiral jets, in festoons, in clustering bunches, in columns and in sheets, all commingled, and uniting as it were by the vehement flames beneath.

The crash of such a tremendous fire must have been appalling, but the wind and the peculiar conditions of the atmosphere did not permit the sound to produce any great effect in our camp.

The iron storm tore over the Russian lines, tossing up, as if in sport, jets of earth and dust, rending asunder gabions, and 'squelching' the parapets, or dashing in amongst the houses and ruins in their rear.

The terrible files of this flying army extending about four miles in front, rushed across the plain, carrying death and terror in their train, swept with heavy and irresistible wings the Russian flanks, and searched their centre to the core. A volley so startling, simultaneous, and tremendously powerful, was probably never before discharged since cannon was introduced. The Russians seemed, for a while, utterly paralysed . . . ◉

The last great battle for Sebastopol had started.

Reeling from the shock of the sudden attack the Russians were slow to retaliate; but after a while retaliate they did, firing 'slowly and with precision, as if they could not afford to throw away an ounce of powder'.

The French, backed up by the British, pressed harder.

All that day the guns boomed out. The Redan and Malakoff fortresses fell silent, their parapets 'all pitted with shot and shell and the sides of the embrasures greatly injured, so that the gabions were sticking out and dislodged in all directions'.

Night fell, and still the bombardment went on.

⊙ There was not one instant in which the shells did not whistle through the air; not a moment in which the sky was not seamed by their fiery curves or illuminated by their explosion; the lines of the Russian earth-works of the Redan, Malakoff, and of all their batteries, were rendered plainly visible by the constant light of the innumerable explosions . . . ⊙

The next night, too, a steady fire was kept up all along the front, with a view to preventing the Russians from repairing damage, and at 5.30 a.m. on September 7th 'the whole of the batteries from Quarantine to Inkerman began their fire with a grand crash . . .'

There was panic, now, in Sebastopol. The Russians began strengthening their position on the north side . . . 'throwing up batteries, dragging guns into position and preparing to defend themselves should they be obliged to leave the city'.

The allies gave them no peace. Once the bombardment began, 150,000 rounds of ammunition were discharged each night.

Storming of the Malakoff (Drawing by Gustav Dore)

It was too much for the beleaguered city.

⊙ The contest on which the eyes of Europe had been turned so long—the event on which the hopes of so many mighty empires depended—was all but determined.

A dull, strange silence, broken at distant intervals by the crash of citadels and palaces as they were blown to dust, succeeded to the incessant dialogue of the cannon which had spoken so loudly and so angrily throughout the entire year . . .

Tired armies, separated from each other by a sea of fires, rested on their arms, and gazed with various emotions on all that remained of the object of their conflicts . . . ⊙

At mid-day on September 8th the French:

⊙ . . . like a swarm of bees, issued forth from their trenches close to the Malakoff, scrambled up its face and were through the embrasures in the twinkling of an eye.

They crossed the seven metres of ground which separated them from the enemy at a few bounds—they drifted as lightly and quickly as autumn leaves before the wind, battalion after battalion, into the embrasures, and in a minute or two after the head of their column issued from the ditch the tricolour was floating over the Bastion. ⊙

They were not without opposition; from twelve o'clock until past seven the French had to meet, and repulse, repeated attempts by the Russians to recapture the Malakoff; but in the end, at considerable cost to both sides, like the Mamelon it was held.

Once again it fell to the British to attack the Redan. As soon as the tricolour was seen above the smoke and dust of the Malakoff, four rockets were sent up as a signal for their assault.

Unbelievably, after so much experience of disaster, the British Generals sent fewer than 1,500 men into the attack. (The French had assembled 36,000 for the attack on the Malakoff.) And this time, of course, the Russians were expecting them.

⊙ Scarcely had the men left the fifth parallel when the guns on the flanks of the Redan opened upon them as they moved up rapidly to the salient, in which there was of course no cannon, as the nature of such a work does not permit of their being placed in that position.

In a few seconds Brigadier Shirley was temporarily blinded by the dust and by earth knocked into his eyes by a shot. He was obliged to retire, and his place was taken by Lieutenant Colonel Bunbury who was next in rank to Colonel Unett, already struck down and carried to the rear.

Brigadier Van Straubenzee received a contusion on the face, and was also forced to leave the field.

Colonel Handcock fell mortally wounded in the head by a bullet and never spoke again.

Colonel Hammond fell dead, Major Welsford was killed on the spot, as he entered the work through an embrasure. Captain Grove was severely wounded . . . ⊙

On they went, grimly and bravely, through the outer defences; into the ditch, over the parapet, through the embrasure. The salient—the narrow point of the fortress projecting out from the city walls—was stormed, and what was left of the British contingent were at last inside the Redan . . .

Crowded together in the narrow confines of the salient they were forced to advance 'by driblets' against a ferocious defence.

⊙ As the alarm of an assault circulated, the enemy came rushing up from the barracks in rear of the Redan, increasing the force and intensity of their fire, while our soldiers dropped fast.

In vain the officers, by voice and act, by example and daring valour, tried to urge our soldiers on to clear the work. The men, most of whom belonged to regiments which had suffered in the trenches, and were acquainted with the

The attack on the Redan

traditions of June 18th (the previous assault on the Redan) had an impression that the Redan was extensively mined and that if they advanced they would all be blown up; yet, to their honour be it recorded many of them acted as became the men of Alma and Inkerman, and, rushing confusedly to the front, were swept down by the enemy's fire.

The officers fell on all sides, singled out as a mark for the enemy by their courage. ⊙

Courage there undoubtedly was, among both men and officers, but the usual disorder and muddle neutralised their efforts.

⊙ The men of the different regiments got mingled together in inextricable confusion. The 19th did not care for the orders of the officers of the 88th, nor did the soldiers of the

23rd heed the commands of an officer who did not belong to
the regiment. The officers could not find their men—the men
had lost sight of their own officers. All the Brigadiers save
Colonel Windham were wounded, or rendered unfit for the
guidance of the attack.

Every moment our men were diminishing in numbers,
while the Russians were arriving in swarms from the town,
and rushing down from the Malakoff, which had been
occupied by the French.

Thrice did Colonel Windham despatch officers to Sir W.
Codrington* . . . to entreat him to send up supports in some
sort of formation; but all these officers were wounded as they
passed from the ditch of the Redan to the rear, and the
Colonel's aide-de-camp, Lieutenant Swire of the 17th, a gallant young officer, was hit dangerously in the hip as he went
on his perilous errand.

Supports were, indeed, sent up, but they advanced in disorder, from the fire to which they were exposed on their way,
and arrived in driblets on the parapet, only to increase the
confusion and carnage.

The narrow neck of the salient was too close to allow of any
kind of formation; and the more the men crowded into it,
the worse was the disorder, and the more they suffered from
the enemy's fire.

The miserable work lasted for an hour . . . ⊙

At last, in desperation, Colonel Windham himself braved the
journey back to ask General Codrington for more help—more
men. The Commander of the Light Division hesitated. The
Colonel urged him, anxiously, assuring him that if the men
kept to their formation the Redan could be won.

⊙ . . . but he spoke too late—for at that very moment our
men were seen leaping into the ditch or running down the
parapet of the salient and through the embrasures out of the

* Commander of the Light Division, successor to Sir George Brown

Inside the Redan

work into the ditch, the Russians following them with the
bayonet and with heavy musketry, and even throwing stones
and grape-shot at them as they lay in the ditch.

The struggle that ensued was short, desperate, and bloody.
Our soldiers, taken at every disadvantage, met the enemy
with the bayonet too, and isolated combats occurred in which
the brave fellows who stood their ground had to defend themselves against three or four adversaries at once.

In this melee the officers, armed only with their swords,
had but little chance; nor had those who carried pistols much
opportunity of using them in such a close and sudden contest.
But the solid weight of the advancing mass, urged on and fed
each moment from the rear by company after company, and
battalion after battalion, prevailed at last against the
isolated and disjointed band, which had abandoned that protection which unanimity of courage affords and had lost the

advantages of discipline and obedience.

Bleeding, panting, and exhausted, our men lay in heaps in the ditch beneath the parapet, sheltered themselves behind stones and in bomb craters . . . or tried to pass back to our advanced parallel and sap, having run the gauntlet of a tremendous fire.

The scene in the ditch was appalling . . . the dead and dying, the wounded and the uninjured were all lying in piles together. The Russians came out of the embrasures, plied them with stones, grape-shot, and the bayonet but were soon forced to retire by the fire of our batteries and riflemen, and under cover of this fire a good many of our men escaped to the approaches.

General Pelissier observed the failure of our attack from the rear of the Malakoff, and sent over to General Simpson to ask if he intended to renew it. The English Commander-in-Chief is reported to have replied that he did not then feel in a condition to do so.

All this time the Guards and Highlanders, the Third and Fourth Divisions, and most of the reserves, had not been engaged. They could, indeed, have furnished materials for making another assault; but the subsequent movements of the Russians render it doubtful whether the glory of carrying the Redan and of redeeming the credit of our arms would not have been dearly purchased by the effusion of more valuable blood.

As soon as we abandoned the assault, the firing slackened along our front; but in the rear of the Malakoff there was a fierce contest going on between masses of Russians, released from the Redan or drawn from the town, and the French inside the work; and the fight for the Little Redan, on the proper left of the Malakoff, was raging furiously.

Clouds of smoke and dust obstructed the view, but the rattle of musketry was incessant and betokened the severe nature of the struggle below. Through the breaks in the smoke there could be seen now and then a tricolour, surmounted by an eagle, fluttering bravely over the inner parapet of the Malakoff.

The storm of battle rolled fiercely round it and beat against it; but it was sustained by strong arms and stout hearts, and all the assaults of the enemy were vain against it.

We could see, too, our noble allies swarming over into the Malakoff, from their splendid approaches to it from the Mamelon; or rushing with speed towards the right, where the Russians, continually reinforced, sought to beat back their foes, and to regain the key of their position.

General Simpson remained in the Green Hill Battery till six o'clock, at which hour General Pelissier sent to inform him that the Malakoff was perfectly safe, and to ask him what the English intended to do with respect to the Redan.

General Simpson had by this time, it is said, formed the determination of attacking it the following morning at five o'clock with the Guards and the Third and Fourth Division. (The difficulty of obtaining accurate information of the progress of an action cannot be better exemplified than by this fact, that at 3 o'clock one of our Generals of Division did not know whether we had taken the Redan or not.)

Towards dusk, the Guards who had been placed in reserve behind our Right Attack, were marched off to their camp, and a portion of the Highlanders were likewise taken off the ground. ⊙

Once again, the French had scored a resounding victory, while the British had suffered a humiliating defeat.

They were not even to have the chance, next day, of redemption.

21
Sebastopol—on fire from the sea to Dockyard Creek

September 1855 ☉ There was a feeling of deep depression in camp all night. We were painfully aware that our attack had failed. The camp was full of wounded men; the hospitals were crowded; and sad stories ran from mouth to mouth respecting the losses of the officers and the behaviour of the men.

Fatigued and worn out by excitement I lay down to rest, but scarcely to sleep. About eleven o'clock my hut was shaken by a violent shock as of an earthquake, but I was so thoroughly tired and worn out that it did not rouse me for more than an instant; having persuaded myself it was 'only a magazine', I was asleep again.

When I rose before daybreak and got up to Cathcart's Hill, there were not many officers standing on that favourite spot; and the sleepers, who had lain down to rest doubtful of the complete success of the French, and certain of our own failure, little dreamt that Sebastopol was ours.

About midnight, the silence having attracted the attention of our men, some volunteers crept up an embrasure of the Redan and found the place deserted by all save the dead and dying.

Soon afterwards, wandering fires gleamed through the streets and outskirts of the town—point after point became alight—the flames shone out of the windows of the houses—rows of mansions caught and burned up, and before daybreak the town of Sebastopol—that fine and stately mistress of the Euxine, on which we had so often turned a longing eye—was on fire from the sea to the Dockyard Creek.

Fort Alexander was blown up early in the night, with a stupendous crash that made the very earth reel. At sunrise, four large explosions on the left followed in quick succession, and announced the destruction of the Quarantine Fort, and of the magazines of the batteries of the Central Bastion and Flagstaff Fort.

In a moment afterwards the Redan was the scene of a very heavy explosion which must have destroyed a number of wounded men on both sides.

The Flagstaff and Garden Batteries blew up, one after another, at 4.45. At 5.30 there were two of the largest and grandest explosions on the left that ever shook the earth— most probably from Fort Alexander and the Grand Magazine.

The rush of black smoke, grey and white vapour, masses of stone, beams of timber, and masonry into the air was appalling, and then followed the roar of a great bombardment; it was a magazine of shells blown up into the air, and exploding like some gigantic pyrotechnic display in the sky—innumerable flashes of fire twittering high up in the column of dark smoke over the town and then changing rapidly into as many balls of white smoke, like little clouds.

All this time the Russians were marching with sullen tramp across the bridge (spanning the harbour, connecting Sebastopol with the northern shore) and boats were busy carrying off stores from the town, or bearing men to the south side, to complete the work of destruction and renew the fires of hidden mines or light up untouched houses.

Of the fleet, all that remained visible were eight steamers and the masts of sunken line-of-battle ships.

As soon as it was dawn the French began to steal from the trenches into the burning town, undismayed by the flames, by the terrors of these explosions, by the fire of a lurking enemy, or by that of their own guns, which kept on slowly discharging cannon-shot and grape into the suburbs at regular intervals, possibly with the very object of deterring stragglers from risking their lives. But the red breeches and the blue breeches, kepi and Zouave fez, could soon be distinguished amid the flames, moving from house to house.

Before five o'clock there were numbers of men coming back with plunder, such as it was, and Russian relics were offered for sale in camp before the Russian battalions had marched out of the city.

The sailors, too, were not behindhand in looking for 'loot', and Jack could be seen staggering under chairs, tables, and lumbering old pictures, through every street and making his way back to the trenches with vast accumulations of worthlessness.

As the rush from camp became very great and everyone sought to visit the Malakoff and the Redan, which were filled with dead and dying men, a line of English cavalry was posted across the front from our extreme left to the French right. They were stationed in all the ravines and roads to the town and trenches with orders to keep back all persons

Cartoon—'RELICS OF THE SIEGE'
Ben. 'I say, Jack!—Give us a lift down with these here *bloodstained Ruins* from Sebasterpol!'

except the generals and staff, and officers and men on duty, and to stop all our men returning with plunder from the town and to take it from them.

As they did not stop the French or Turks or Sardinians, this order gave rise to a good deal of grumbling, particularly when a man, after lugging a heavy chair several miles, or a table, or some such article, was deprived of it by our sentries. ⊙

Resentful though he might be of this discrimination, the British soldier seems to have borne no grudge against his French comrade and with, in the circumstances, commendable generosity, showed his admiration for his courage and success:

⊙ It so happened that as the remnants of the French regiments engaged on the left against the Malakoff and Little Redan marched to their tents in the morning, our Second Division was drawn up on the parade ground in front of their camp, and the French had to pass their lines.

The instant the leading regiment of Zouaves came up to the spot where our first regiment was placed, the men, with one spontaneous burst, rent the air with an English cheer.

The French officers drew their swords, their men dressed up and marched past as if at a review, while regiment after regiment of the Second Division caught up the cry, and at last our men presented arms to their brave comrades of France, the officers on both sides saluted with their swords, and this continued till the last man had marched by.

Mingled with the plunderers from the front were many wounded men. The ambulances never ceased—now moving heavily and slowly with their burdens, again rattling at a trot to the front for a fresh cargo—and the ground between the trenches and the camp was studded with cacolets or mule litters.

Already the funeral parties had commenced their labours. Moving down on the right flank of our cavalry pickets, a small party of us managed to turn them cleverly, and to get out among the French works between the Mamelon and Malakoff. The ground was here literally paved with shot and shell, and the surface was deeply honeycombed by the explosions of bombs at every square yard. ⊙

Inside the Malakoff the sight was 'too terrible to dwell upon'.

⊙ The French are carrying away their own and the Russian wounded, and there are four distinct piles of dead formed to clear the way. The ground is marked by pools of blood, and the smell is already noisome; swarms of flies settle on dead and dying; broken muskets, torn clothes, caps, shakos, swords, bayonets, bags of bread, canteens and haversacks are lying in indescribable confusion all over the place, mingled with heaps of shot, of grape, bits of shell, cartridges, case and canister, loose powder, official papers and cooking tins . . . ⊙

Russell explored the fortress with characteristic thoroughness, and discovered descending tunnels below the parapet, leading down to a series of rooms which provided a sort of primitive air-raid shelter, eight to ten feet square and four to five feet high, covered over with layer upon layer of protective material—mainly ships' masts and earth.

Here, apparently, the garrison 'went to ground' during heavy bombardments.

'The odour of these narrow chambers,' Russell informed his readers, 'is villainous, and the air reeks with blood and abominations unutterable'. He went on:

⊙ In one of these dungeons, which is excavated in the solid rock, and was probably underneath the old White Tower, the officer commanding seems to have lived.

It must have been a dreary residence. The floor and the entrance were littered a foot deep with reports, returns, and perhaps dispatches assuring the Czar that the place had sustained no damage.

221

The destruction of Sebastopol, seen from the Redan heights
(from a sketch made on the morning of September 9th, 1855)

The garrison were in these narrow chambers enjoying their siesta, which they invariably take at twelve o'clock, when the French burst in on them like a torrent and, as it were, drowned them in their holes. ⊙

The ditch outside the Malakoff, to the north:

⊙ . . . was yet full of French and Russians piled over each other in horrid confusion. On the right, towards the Little Redan, the ground was literally strewn with bodies as thick as they could lie, and in the ditch they were piled over each other. . . . The Russians lay inside the work in heaps like carcases in a butcher's cart, and the wounds, the blood—the sight, exceeded all I had hitherto witnessed.

Descending from the Malakoff, we come upon a suburb of ruined houses open to the sea—it is filled with dead. The Russians had crept away into holes and corners in every

222

house, to die like poisoned rats; artillery horses with their entrails torn open by shot were stretched all over the space at the back of the Malakoff, marking the place where the Russians moved up their last column to re-take it under the cover of a heavy field battery.

Every house, the church, some public buildings, sentry-boxes—all alike were broken and riddled by cannon and mortar. ⊙

A few days later Russell sent Delane a package containing a few souvenirs from the ruins—a fragment of stone from the Governor's house, a bit of the dockyard wall, and some laburnum seeds from the garden round the Church of St Peter and St Paul.

From the suburb he went on to explore the dockyard, claimed by some to be unequalled in the world.

⊙ Gates and store sides are splintered and pierced by shot. There are the stately dockyard buildings on the right, which used to look so clean and white and spruce. Parts of them are knocked to atoms, and hang together in such shreds and patches that it is only wonderful they cohere. ⊙

But the most horrific sights were yet to come.

⊙ Of all the pictures of the horrors of war which have ever been presented to the world, the hospital of Sebastopol offered the most heart-rending and revolting.

The building used as an hospital was inside the dockyard wall and peculiarly exposed to the action of shot and shell bounding over the Redan. It bore in sides, roof, windows, and doors, frequent and distinctive proofs of the severity of the cannonade.

Entering one of these doors, I beheld such a sight as few men, thank God, have ever witnessed.

In a long, low room, supported by square pillars arched at the top, and dimly lighted through shattered and unglazed window-frames, lay the wounded Russians.

The wounded, did I say? No, but the dead—the rotten and festering corpses of the soldiers, who were left to die in their extreme agony, untended, uncared for, packed as close as they could be stowed, some on the floor, others on wretched trestles and bedsteads or pallets of straw, sopped and saturated with blood which oozed and trickled through upon the floor, mingling with the droppings of corruption.

With the roar of exploding fortresses in their ears—with shells and shot pouring through the roof and sides of the rooms in which they lay—with the crackling and hissing of fire around them, these poor fellows, who had served their loving friend and master the Czar but too well, were consigned to their terrible fate.

Many might have been saved by ordinary care. Many, nearly mad by the scene around them, or seeking escape from it in their extremest agony, had rolled away under the beds and glared out on the heart-stricken spectator.

Many, with legs and arms broken and twisted, the jagged splinters sticking through the raw flesh, implored aid, water, food, or pity; or, deprived of speech by the approach of death or by dreadful injuries in the head or trunk, pointed to the lethal spot. Many seemed bent alone on making their peace with Heaven.

The attitudes of some were so hideously fantastic as to root one to the ground by a sort of dreadful fascination. The bodies of numbers of men were swollen and bloated to an incredible degree; and the features distended to a gigantic size with eyes protruding from the sockets and the blackened tongue lolling out of the mouth, compressed tightly by the teeth, which had set upon it in the death-rattle, made one shudder and reel round. ☉

Shaken, and sickened, Russell went on to the Great Redan, scene of the British army's bitter disappointment and defeat. Things were no better here.

☉ All the houses behind it a mass of broken stones—a

clock turret, with a shot right through the clock; a pagoda in ruins; another clock-tower with all the clock destroyed save the dial, with the words 'Barwise, London' thereon; cookhouses, where human blood was running among the utensils; in one place a shell had lodged in the boiler and blown it and its contents, and probably its attendants, to pieces. Everywhere wreck and destruction.

Climbing up to the Redan, which was fearfully cumbered with the dead, we witnessed the scene of the desperate attack and defence which cost both sides so much blood.

The ditch outside made one sick—it was piled up with English dead, some of them scorched and blackened by the explosion, and others lacerated beyond recognition.

The quantity of broken gabions and gun-carriages here was extraordinary; the ground was covered with them. The bomb-proofs were the same as in the Malakoff, and in one of them a music-book was found with a woman's name in it, and a canary bird and vase of flowers were outside the entrance. ⊙

The Russians made one last, sad, spectacular gesture of dignified defiance—of self-immolation. Only too aware that the allies' next move would be to destroy the remnants of their navy, they took matters into their own hands.

In the early hours of the morning less than two days after the final battle, under the very eyes of the Naval Brigade detailed to carry out the destruction, one of the Russian ships crept close inshore.

⊙ A broad light was perceived in her fore hatchway. The leading steamer on the opposite side in a second afterwards exhibited gleams of equal brightness, and then one! two! three! four! five!—as though from signal guns the remaining steamers, with one exception, emitted jets of fire from their bows.

The jets soon became columns of flame and smoke—the wind blew fresh and strong, and the night was dark, so that the fire spread with rapidity along the vessels, and soon lighted up the whole of the northern heavens.

The masts were speedily licked and warmed into a fiery glow and the rigging burst out into fitful wavering lines of light, struggling with the wind for life: the yards shed lambent showers of spark and burning splinters upon the water.

The northern works could be readily traced by the light of the conflagration, and the faces of the Russian soldiers and sailors who were scattered about on the face of the cliff shone out now and then, and justified Rembrandt.

The work of destruction sped rapidly. The vessels were soon nothing but huge arks of blinding light, which hissed and crackled fiercely and threw up clouds of sparks and embers; and the guns, as they became hot, exploded, and shook the crazy hulls to atoms.

One after another they went down into the seething waters . . . ⊙

The next morning the last of the Russian ships was 'cleverly scuttled', with no interference from the allies. Nor was any attempt made to interfere when the Russians began an orderly retreat to the north bank of the Tchernaya estuary.

⊙ He led his battalions in narrow files across the deep arm of the sea, which ought to have been commanded by our guns, and in the face of the most powerful fleet. He actually paraded them in our sight as they crossed, and carried off all his most useful stores and munitions of war.

He sank his ships and blew up his forts without molestation; nothing was done to harass him in his retreat, with the exception of some paltry efforts to break down the bridge by cannon-shot, or to shell the troops as they marched over.

His steamers towed his boats across at their leisure, and when every man had been placed in safety, and not till then, the Russians began to dislocate and float off the different portions of their bridge, and to pull it over to the north side. ◉

It was almost as though the allies were mesmerised . . . paralysed. Inert, they watched as the enemy, getting their second wind, 'calmly strengthened their position on the north side' until 'the face of the country bristled with their cannon and their batteries'!

◉ Day and night the roar of their guns sounded through our camp, and occasionally equalled the noise of the old cannonades, which we hoped had died into silence for ever.

There was no sign of any intention on their part to abandon a position on which they had lavished so much care and labour. In their new position they had placed between themselves and us a deep arm of the sea, a river, and the sides of a plateau as steep as a wall.

We permitted them to get off at their leisure, and looked on, while the Russian battalions filed over the narrow bridge, emerging in unbroken order out of that frightful sea of raging fire and smoke which was tossed up into billows of flame by the frequent explosion of great fortresses and magazines.

At what moment our generals woke up and knew what was going on I cannot tell, but it is certain they did not, as a body, distress themselves by any violent efforts to get a near view of the enemy's movements *early* in the morning.

Why did not the English move? Orders and counter-orders were sent day after day—requisitions on Captain This to know how many mules he had to carry ball cartridge; orders to Captain That to turn out his battery for the purpose of taking the field at daybreak the next morning; counter-orders in the evening re-countered and retracted at night, till it was hard to say what was to be done; and if the men who gave the commands were in half as confused a state of mind as those who received them, they were indeed in a pitiable plight. The work of the army was actually that of preparation not for motion, but for stagnation . . . ◉

Once more the allies had lost—had thrown away it seemed

227

almost wilfully—the chance to finish off the Russians.

In a dispatch dated September 14th Russell reminded readers of *The Times* of an anniversary . . . and of much more than that:

⊙ It is just one year to this day since we landed at Calamita Bay. In that time we have stormed the heights of the Alma, sustained the glorious disaster of Balaklava, fought the great fight of Inkerman, swept the Sea of Azov and its seaboard, wasted Kertch, and seized upon Yenikale—have witnessed the battle of the Tchernaya—have opened seven bombardments upon Sebastopol—have held in check every general and every soldier that Russia could spare; and now, after the endurance of every ill that an enemy at home and abroad could inflict upon us—after passing through the summer's heat and winter's frost—after being purged in the fire of sickness and death, repulse and disaster, and above all in the fiery glow of victory, the British standard floats above Sebastopol. ⊙

Judging by his reports of the state of Sebastopol, it was a hollow victory. And few of the men who had landed at Calamita Bay a year before had lived to see even that.

22
Nor did his comrade stop to mourn his death

September 1855. Now that Sebastopol had fallen—the original goal achieved—what was the army to do?

Nobody seemed to know. The roads and railway were improved against the coming winter, vast quantities of stores were brought in; Sebastopol was raided for what was left of its 'furniture, fixtures and fittings'.

◉ Doors, windows, locks, hinges, fire-places, stoves, pictures, chairs, tables, beams of wood, roofing, ceiling, flooring, sheet-lead, rolled copper, cut stone, crockery, and innumerable articles of every description were brought up by carts, horses, ponies, and by men, every day in great quantities; and were found most useful in the construction and ornamentation of our huts.

There were very few officers who had not got some trophies; arms of various description, great-coats, and helmets, pictures of saints—often embellished by the finders with grotesque adornments of moustachios, short pipes, and eye-glasses—and portraits of the Czar which had not quite escaped the spirit of improvement manifested by our soldiery, were very common.

Many articles of English workmanship abounded—and canary birds sang and flowers bloomed amid the murky horrors of these blood-stained casements. ◉

The soldiers, of course, did the hard, physical work. The officers had very little to do, and:

◉ . . . found it difficult to kill time, riding about Sebastopol, visiting Balaklava, foraging at Kamiesch, or hunting for quail, which were occasionally found in swarms all over the steppe and formed most grateful additions to the mess table. ◉

The one great British victory—Alma—was celebrated on September 20th, with 'Alma dinners', and the distribution of medals, clasps and 'ribands'. The design of these was strongly criticised, the ribbon being judged 'unbecoming' and the clasp 'likened generally to the labels on public house wine bottles'.

Russell, ever jealous of the reputation of the true fighting man, was critical also of the method of distributing war medals.

◉ The Light Division, I believe, paraded and received

229

Punch cartoon—'PATIENT HEROES'

'WELL, JACK! HERE'S GOOD NEWS FROM HOME. WE'RE TO HAVE
A MEDAL.'

'THAT'S VERY KIND. MAYBE ONE OF THESE DAYS WE'LL HAVE
A COAT TO STICK IT ON!'

their medals and clasps . . . *en masse*, with some show of
ceremony. Perhaps the John Smith alluded to never saw a
shot fired except at the distance of several miles. He might
have been on peaceful guard at Lord Raglan's headquarters
on the 5th of November; yet he wears the clasp for Inkerman.
He might have been engaged in no more sanguinary work
than that of killing oxen and sheep for the division in the
commissariat slaughter-house, and yet he will show on his
breast 'Crimea' (of course), 'Alma', 'Balaklava', 'Inkerman'.

Our wretched system of bestowing decorations on classes,
and sowing them broadcast over a whole army, deprives
them of much of their real value. What can a survivor of the
Light Cavalry charge think of the clasp 'Balaklava' when he
sees whole divisions of infantry soldiers wearing the name on
their breasts? ◉

It was not the first time Russell had pondered the significance—or lack of it—of war-medals. Several months earlier he had suggested that one should be especially struck for acts of true valour. He had even suggested that it should carry the name 'Victoria'. A year later the Order of the Victoria Cross was established. It was probably a coincidence —Russell never claimed to have been its inspiration—but it nevertheless gave him pleasure that his idea had borne fruit.

He had plenty of time during the lull which followed the fall of Sebastopol to look back over the year he had spent with the army in the Crimea, and he continued to mourn lost comrades.

But there was no profit in fighting old battles. The war was not over yet—though there was to be no more action on the scale of Alma, Balaklava, Inkerman, Tchernaya or the assaults on the bastions of Sebastopol, and there were rumours everywhere of 'peace before Christmas'.

September/October 1855. There was to be one last confrontation; an operation not unlike the expedition to Kertch, though this time the object was to paralyse the great shipyard, dock area, and naval arsenal at Nicolaev in the Russian Ukraine.

Two small forts which guarded the entrance to the waterway on which Nicolaev stands were the principal objectives.

The expedition left on October 7th and anchored off Odessa, sixty miles south-east of Nicolaev, in the Black Sea. Odessa was not, of course, the target, but the allies hoped 'to fill the minds of the authorities with apprehensions of a descent upon the town after a general bombardment and to induce them to withdraw their troops from the neighbourhood. of the place we are going to attack'.

It worked. The town, which at first had looked 'as peaceful as a drop scene at the theatre' sprang to the alert.

⊙ As the first ship of the English squadron cast anchor, a long line of dust was observed rising over the hilly coast to the north of Odessa, and by the beach . . . we soon made out bayonets glistening in the sun, and a strong body of Russian infantry, with field-pieces and baggage, consisting of some five or six thousand men, marching in all haste towards the city . . . ⊙

Nothing happened. The allied fleet lay quietly at anchor, having achieved its first objective without firing a shot.

⊙ The evening passed quietly; the Admiral made but few signals, but it was known that tomorrow nothing would be done, and that till the work of sounding off Kinburn (one of the two forts) and laying down buoys for the fleet had been accomplished, the attack would not come off. ⊙

In fact the fleet was fog-bound for the next two days. It cleared on October 11th, but still no move was made. It was not until October 15th that troops landed three miles west of Kinburn Fort—'without the smallest opposition, or even the appearance of an enemy'.

After a day of consolidation, dawn on the 17th broke dull and grey, with wind off the shore and the sea quite calm.

⊙ The fleet was perfectly still, but the mortar-vessels, floating-batteries, and gun boats were getting up steam, and before nine o'clock they might be seen leaving the rest of the armada, and making for the south side of the fort.

The floating-batteries opened with a magnificent crash at 9.30 a.m. and one in particular distinguished itself for the regularity, precision, and weight of its fire throughout the day.

The enemy replied with alacrity, and his batteries must have been put to a severe test, for the water was splashed into pillars by shot all over them.

At 11.10 a fire broke out in the long barrack, and speedily spread from end to end of the fort, driving the artillerymen from their guns. Small explosions of supply ammunition took

232

place inside. ⊙

The Russians fought bravely, almost desperately, but the weight of the allied attack was too much for them. At a quarter past eleven the Russian 'Jack'* was shot away. Not very long afterwards:

⊙ . . . a flag was waved from the parapet, and two boats, each bearing a flag of truce, pushed off, one from the English and another from the French, Admiral, and at the same time Sir Houston Steward proceeded to land near the battery, where he found the French General advancing to parley with the Governor.

Major-General Kokonovitch advanced with a sword and pistol in one hand and a pistol in the other. He threw down his sword at the officer's feet, and discharged his pistols into the ground . . . in token of surrender.

He was moved to tears, and as he left the fort turned round and uttered some passionate exclamation in Russian, of which the interpreter could only make out 'Oh Kinburn! Kinburn! Glory of Suvorov and my shame, I abandon you,' or something to that effect.

As the garrison marched out they were ordered to pile their arms, but many of them threw them on the ground at the feet of the conquerors, with rage and mortification depicted on their features.

Kokonovitch wept as he threw down the pen with which he signed the articles of surrender, but he had no reason to be ashamed of his defence . . . ⊙

There was no need to fight for the second of the two forts, the one below Oczakoff. On the 18th October the Russians set it on fire and blew up the magazines. The next day a French boat left the Rear Admiral's ship with a flag of truce.

⊙ As the boat neared the beach, an officer followed by two soldiers came down from the town to meet them. One of the men bore a tremendous flag of truce—a large tablecloth

* Flag

suspended from a long pole, under the weight of which he staggered as he walked. ⊙

A letter was handed over by the French, reporting that forty-five wounded Russians were in the French ambulances at Kinburn. This done, the Russian standard-bearer retired, 'his tablecloth waving behind him'.

October/November 1855. The Crimean War was virtually at an end. And it was fitting, somehow, that it should end on such a ludicrous note. The gallant noise of drums and trumpets—even the groans and shrieks of agony—of the early months had tailed away almost to a whimper.

A short foray by a few of the allied ships into the estuary of the River Bug (the waterway guarded by the twin fortresses of Kinburn and Oczakoff) was never pressed home; at last someone in charge of operations had the wit to see how unproductive it would be to pit the ships' guns against shore emplacements sited on cliffs a hundred feet high, on both sides of the river.

With what dignity it could muster, the expedition withdrew, and returned to its anchorage off the Bug; 'and remained there for the night, without the smallest apprehensions that the enemy could do us any harm from Nicholaev'.

Had the expedition been larger (as the English had wished) something more might have been achieved; but the entire story of the Crimean War is one of missed opportunities, wrong decisions, inept judgements and futile engagements. A sudden burst of brilliant leadership was hardly likely at this stage.

One of the few who hardly faltered throughout the whole campaign was Russell himself. He was not, perhaps, always right—and certainly often impulsively tactless—but his energy was unfailing and his powers of observation and criticism never flagged. During the abortive sortie up the River Bug his sharp-eyed gaze was everywhere, taking in as always the small domestic detail, as well as the military scene; and it was the first as much as the second which brought the campaign vividly to life for his readers. They could *see* what was happening, and why, as they read his dispatches. The whole situation leapt into colourful life.

And even at this late stage he was still tireless in his attacks on authority; quick in his own and others' defence. Shortly after his return from the expedition to the Bug he wrote:

⊙ The English journals contain . . . many comments on a statement published in my correspondence describing the ill-fated attack on the Redan on the 8th September, in which the Commander-in-Chief, the Quartermaster-General, and the General of Engineers, were represented as being in the second parallel, sheltering themselves as well as they could from the effects of the dust and of the bitter cold wind which blew throughout the day.

Now, it is very far from my intention to expose the Generals to ridicule. General Simpson came out here as chief of staff to ease Lord Raglan of a load of duties which pressed too heavily upon him, and to neutralize the acids in the Quarter-master-General and the Adjutant-General's Departments.

When Lord Raglan died, the command was thrust upon General Simpson, and he who had served for many anxious years, feeling he was no longer the stout soldier that had won renown for his unaristocratic name in the Peninsula, or as an experienced General, had been regarded as the only successor to a Napier in India, made representations to the Government at home which did credit to his modesty and humility, if not to his judgement.

In fact, he begged of them to place the command in other hands. Well, the Government refused to do so. They left General Simpson Commander-in-Chief of our army in spite of himself, and in defiance of his own diffident remonstrances. Left? No, but forced him—the round peg, as he declared himself to be—into a square hole; and now they are astonished forsooth that the peg did not fit!

Again, is there any good ground for attacking one whose business it is to tell all that is interesting to the British public for saying what the Generals did, where they were placed, and how they appeared?

I cannot answer the question, but it strikes me, if it be answered in the affirmative, the respondent must be the last of the protectionists—the Don Quixote of 'sham', the champion of humbug, and the high priest of national delusion.

Why is the writer to be attacked? Because he exposed these distinguished officers to ridicule and calumny. What, is not a General a human being? If he is cold, must he alone not wear a cloak? If sick, must he alone not avail himself of a litter? If storm-driven, must he alone bear its peltings with uncovered ears?

Are 'distinguished officers' to be always in full uniform—in cocked hats, epaulettes, orders and jackboots, shouting 'Follow me!' to their legions, or taking snuff à la Gomersall and Napoleon, in extreme military crises in front of their battalions?

If they are, they ought not to be; surely, if they ought to be, they are not. ◉

General Simpson was, in fact, replaced as Commander-in-Chief only a few days after Russell had written this dispatch, by Sir William Codrington, who had served in the Crimea since the beginning of the campaign, having left England on the same day as Russell, with the rank of Colonel in the Coldstream Guards.

Russell appeared to be mildly pleased, if not overjoyed, by the choice. Sir William was, he reported, 'just the man to draw in the reins gently but firmly, and to correct the evils which tend to mar (the army's) efficiency in the field'.

There was, he added, a little too much free-and-easiness. Rum was too plentiful, and money too abundant. In short, a vast amount of drinking was going on among the bored, battle-weary, troops.

Not that there was a great deal left for General Sir William Codrington to do. Sebastopol's great docks were destroyed, new roads were laid down—as the winter drew on there was even talk of establishing libraries for those (by no means all) who could read. With no very definite plans for the future the army appeared to be settling in for another winter.

November 1855/April 1856. The autumn had been a fine one, 'of unexceptionable mildness'. 'Storms lowered over us and passed away; dark skies threatened us and melted into floods of golden sunbeams . . .' Russell wrote lyrically as late as November 20th. But no advantage was taken of the good weather, although the physical state of the troops was infinitely better than it had been at the same time the previous year. They were better housed, better fed, and better clothed.

They became, in fact, almost dangerously 'settled in'. Dogs and cats from the devastated city of Sebastopol added an extra touch of domesticity. Even a camel—a 'huge double-humped Bactrian'—arrived out of nowhere and established itself outside Russell's hut.

⊙ Our legs as we went out and in were within easy reach of his prodigious teeth. But he was a good-natured brute and never attempted to bite unless one tried to mount him, when he disgorged his food, and spat it out at the assailant, or snapped his jaws at him . . . ⊙

There was, Russell admitted, very little indeed for him to report at this time, except for a mysterious explosion in the French camp on November 15th, which killed and wounded a large number of British, as well as French, troops. There was little contact with the enemy, apart from the occasional skirmish.

So quiet, and so dull, in fact had the war become that by the beginning of December Russell was planning a holiday in England. The decision was not taken without hesitation. Russell was well aware of the vulnerability of his situation. On December 4th he wrote to his wife:

⊙ Right or wrong, I'll leave camp as soon as Hardman [his substitute] arrives. I say 'right or wrong' for many reasons which men can see, but which women perhaps cannot be expected to appreciate.

Just for example, suppose this: *The Times* now think me invaluable; I cost them a great deal, the fame of their correspondence is good—a new man, quite as good a writer as myself, takes my place; they find he answers admirably and that it is the occasion makes the writer, and I, who am becoming too big for them, am shelved.

Again, I get the name of being a 'runaway' because I fear another winter, and I can never write a word against the officers who flock home on 'private affairs'.

Again, I have many friends whose acquaintance I could cultivate during the dark social evenings of winter but whose society is impossible during the active operations.

Again, I run a great expense.

Again, *we must be parted once more*. That is the great reason of all . . . ⊙

In spite of all this, he decided to go. 'If I start on Thursday, the 13th,' he went on in his letter, 'that will just land me home on Christmas Day. I can scarcely believe it—it's like a dream . . .'

One worry, at least, was unfounded. However good a writer Russell's substitute, as a personality he was, and could not be, replaced as the chronicler of the Crimean War. And anyway, there was really no more war to write about. In a dispatch dated January 1st, 1856, Hardman wrote:

◉ There can hardly be a more perfect example of a sine-cure than the office of a newspaper correspondent in the camp before Sebastopol at the present time. No man's occupation was ever more completely gone. He may lay his pen upon the shelf with a quiet conscience—nay, he must do so, unless he resign himself to chronicle the small beer of the camp.

As to finding anything of importance to write about, it is out of the question . . . ◉

Back in England, with just such a 'quiet conscience', Russell enjoyed his holiday; meeting friends, going to the theatre, eating good meals in comfortable surroundings, basking in the glow of fame. 'Balaklava Russell', they called him —and anything, but anything, he wanted was his.

Charles Kean, the actor-manager, wrote to him:

◉ Be assured I shall be too happy to place any accommodation my theatre can afford at your disposal any night (or every night) you can pay me a visit. If you will only let me know what evening you are at liberty for the purpose, I shall be delighted to forward a Box card. It is but a small return for the many hours of gratification and interest I have derived from reading your admirable letters from the Crimea.

I only wish it were in my power to afford a better proof of my high appreciation of your great talents. ◉

In fact the only fly in Russell's holiday enjoyment was the necessity to explain his 'accounts' to the Manager of *The Times*—a task so difficult that in the end Mowbray Morris threw up his hands, wiped the slate clean, and started again; with the stern request that in future Russell should 'render monthly accounts of expenditure, showing a clean balance', something Russell was congenitally incapable of doing.

On February 28th, 1856, after a long period when hardly a shot was fired, an Armistice was signed by Russia and the allies; and on April 2nd peace was officially proclaimed.

Russell returned, reluctantly, from London to the Crimea, to cover the withdrawal of the allied troops and the general clearing up.

It was a sad return for him; there would be no more action or excitement, and so many of his friends had died in the attack on the Redan that the camp before Sebastopol was haunted by pitiful ghosts.

He plodded grimly round, reliving old campaigns, watching 'grand reviews', touring the countryside, making pilgrimages to old battlegrounds and graveyards.

The very last words he wrote from the Crimea came from the site of the only British victory: the Alma—a place which drew him back over and over again, like a magnet; a place almost of nostalgia, now that the scent of flowers overwhelmed the stench of blood and powder . . .

June 1856 ◉ The white telegraph station over the river, which stood on the Russian left, can be seen for many miles on a clear day, but on the steppe mirage is very common, and the horizon is rarely well-defined. It is often lost in a fantastic margin resembling the sea-line of an agitated ocean.

Bustards, on the *qui vive* about their young, soar slowly before us, and eagles, vultures, and many species of falcons are visible in pursuit of their prey, which must consist for the most part of hares, which are very large and numerous.

In one of the hollows in the steppe, about three miles from the Alma, there is a small hamlet, but, with this exception, not a habitation is visible over the whole of this vast expanse of land.

It is famous ground for a long canter, or as much of a gallop as your horse will stand; so with the help of an occasional scurry after a hare the distance melts away, and as we go crashing through the sweet flowers, the telegraph rises higher and clearer till we pull up at the foot of the mound on which it stands . . .

There are fifteen large sepulchral mounds around the telegraph, wherein lie French and Russians, and the ravines are still full of bones, and of fragments of clothing and accoutrements.

There is an excellent view of the French position and attack from the edge of the plateau. The enemy must have had every movement of the allies under their eyes from the time they left Bouljanak till they halted to form for battle; and the spectacle could not have been one to have given them much courage, or to have influenced their ardour.

A huge mound, composed of fifteen or sixteen gigantic graves, at the distance of 400 or 500 yards from the river on its north side, denotes the resting place of those who fell before the army crossed the stream, or who died after the fight in the ambulances.

The road by which we advanced to the bridge is just as it was on the 20th September, and on the right, close to the stream, are the blackened ruins of the village of Bourliouk. . . . The bridge has been substantially re-built . . . The old post-house, on the right of the road before you come to the bridge, is about to be reconstructed and a guard of soldiers were lodged in its ruins. It will be, to all appearances, a handsome house when it is finished.

I surveyed its ruins with peculiar interest, for I know a person very intimately who took shelter in this house, part of which was on fire, to get out of a fire still hotter, till he was driven out by a shell falling through the roof; and it was at the wall outside, which is yet torn by shot, that I met the first two wounded officers I saw that day—two officers of the 30th, one hit through the chest or side; the other wounded in the leg or arm.

They were helping each other from the river, bleeding and weak, and I was fortunate enough to be able to bring to their aid a Staff surgeon belonging to the Cavalry Division, who examined their wounds under fire.

Close to this I had previously seen the first man killed—a

drummer, who was carrying a litter and who was struck by a round shot which bowled slowly along the road and hit him, with a peculiar squashing sound, on the hop. He fell, broken in two, and never moved; nor did his comrade, who was carrying the other end of the litter, stop to mourn over his death . . .

All these things, and many more, came back upon me as I looked around. I could recall that narrow road filled with dead and dying—poor young Burgoyne going past on his litter, crying out cheerily, 'It's all right—it's only my foot'; 'Billy Fitzgerald' shot through both legs lying up against the wall, and chatting away as if he had just sat down after a quadrille; a white-haired field-officer (of the 55th) whose name I don't know, badly wounded through the body, who could only moan bitterly, 'Oh, my poor men! Oh, my poor men! They hadn't a chance!'

Then the river stained here and there with blood, still flowing from the dead and dying who lay on the shallows and the banks, lined nevertheless by hundreds who drank its waters eagerly; the horrid procession of the dripping litters, going to the rear of the fight; the solid mass of Adams' brigade, halted by Lord Raglan's orders as it emerged from the smoke of Bourliouk; the Staff itself and the Commander-in-Chief, gathered on the rising ground close by; that ghastly battle-field where so many lay in so small a place putrescent with heat and wounds.

The grey blocks of Russians melting away like clouds, and drifted off by the fierce breath of battle; the shriek and rush of the shells from the brass howitzers in the battery, the patter of the rifle, the rattling roll of the musketry, the frantic cheers of our men as they stood victors on the heights, drowning the groans and cries which for a moment succeeded the roar of battle; the shrill flourish of the French bugles, and the joyous clamour of their drums from the other side of the ravine—all came back upon the ear again, and the eye renewed its pleasure as it gazed from the ridge upon the plain where it had before seen the Russians flying in disorder, with their rear still covered by the threatened squadrons of their cavalry.

I recalled the two days passed as no army ought to pass two days—on the field of battle, amid the dead—the horrid labours of those hours of despondency and grief where all should have been triumph and rejoicing, and the awakened vigour with which the army broke from its bivouac on the Alma and set out with no certain aim, no fixed project, on its chance march which fate has made so successful, and so prosperous . . .

In the ditch of the fieldwork there are about twenty large graves covered with long grass and wild flowers. The trench is about 150 yards long, and it is filled with earth which has tumbled down into it from the parapet; the traces of the embrasures still remain. There are two stone crosses erected inside the trench on heaps of dead.

This is all that remains to betoken the scene of the action on our side, except a few pieces of threadbare rags and bits of accoutrement, leather straps, old shakoes, and fragments of cowhide knapsacks.

Some miserable Tartars prowl about the ruins of Bourliouk to act as unintelligible guides, and to pick up the fragments left after the river-side meal of the visitors.

Starting at six o'clock a.m. one can get to the Alma, spend three hours there and return to camp in time for dinner with the greatest ease, if one has a good horse. It is under fifty miles.

The last time I was there I threw a fly over the waters, having heard that there were trout in the stream, but only a few 'logger-headed chub' and a kind of dace, responded to the effort.

And so I take leave of this little river, which shall henceforth be celebrated in history to the end of time. ◉

Postscript:
What would have come of it all
had I followed the quiet path?

Russell went out to the Crimea an unknown newspaper reporter, regarded with hostility and suspicion by many in authority. He returned, still an object of resentment to some, but to the vast majority a hero. After all, he had exposed not only the horrors and blunders, but the heroism, self-sacrifice, fortitude and occasional brilliance of the British fighting man, in an era when war was still regarded as a problem-solver and promoter of national glory.

Lord Palmerston, the Prime Minister, invited him to breakfast and asked his advice about the administration of the army. His old university—Trinity College, Dublin—conferred the honorary degree of Doctor of Laws on him. Lecture societies everywhere clamoured to hear him speak.

The old criticisms, of course, rumbled on, but there were many to justify and support his views and actions. John Delane, *The Times*'s shrewd Editor, well aware of both the value of Russell's fame and the quality of his writing, but determined not to appear over-impressed, sent him after only a very short rest to Russia again, to describe a very different event: the Coronation of Czar Alexander II. He was a reporter; the Crimean War had been one 'job', and this was another, the posting implied.

Russell was thirty-three years old when he first embarked for the Crimea. Although it may have seemed a lifetime to him before he returned to England, it was really only the beginning of a career which covered practically every type of reporting. But it was war-reporting which made, and kept, him famous. Among the wars he witnessed were the Indian

Mutiny, the American Civil War, and the Franco-Prussian War.

Wherever he went he was in the thick of the action. He was wounded more than once, and suffered the sort of sickness over-exposure and privation—then even more than now —bring with them. Yet he lived to be almost eighty-seven, and died peacefully in his bed, full not only of years, but also of honours, including, in 1895, a Knighthood.

He left behind a wealth of descriptive writing—letters and diaries in addition to his newspaper dispatches—which bring to startling life half a century of living, as well as dying. This, one feels, was how it really was.

Nor did his influence, and the effect of his words, cease when the newspapers in which his dispatches appeared yellowed with age. Widespread reforms were carried out in the Army in the late nineteenth century. The many overlapping departments which had controlled various parts of the military machine came together under one roof, to form the War Office; the clothing of the troops was no longer left to the whim of Regimental Colonels—a central depot supplied uniforms to all; the famous Enfield factory was established to produce small-arms; training camps were set up for the ranks where all aspects of their profession from barrack-square drill to Gunnery and Musketry were taught by experts, under proper supervision; and there were reforms, too, in welfare, education, recreation and sports.

Camberley Staff College was built for the professional training of officers, and eventually there were changes in the conditions under which commissions were granted and promotion conferred.

A number of other vital lessons were learned in the Crimea, not least the importance of a proper Medical Service. It is difficult to believe that when the troops sailed for Malta early in 1854 there was little provision made for transporting the sick and wounded beyond a handful of stretchers, and no one to carry them except the feeble pensioners who made up the Hospital Conveyance Corps; that one hundred and sixty-three surgeons were expected to cope with all casualties —not only in the Crimea, but wherever British troops were stationed throughout the world!

In 1857, the year after the Crimean War ended, Florence Nightingale began her famous and far-reaching enquiry into the state of health in the British Army. Three years later she opened her training school for nurses at St Thomas's Hospital in London.

'I . . . wonder what would have come of it all had I followed the quiet path . . . instead of those noisy drums and trumpets,' Russell wrote in 1882. History, it is certain, would have been the poorer; and so would the lot of the British soldier and his family.

Reading list

The following is a short list intended for those interested in extending their reading on the subject of this book. It is by no means definitive; once launched, the reader will find an almost endless store of books, each one approaching the War from a different aspect; each throwing more light on, or challenging the assumptions of, another. The author herself consulted many modern, and contemporary, records not listed.

W. H. RUSSELL, *The British Expedition to the Crimea* (1858)

W. H. RUSSELL, *The War*, 2 vols. (London: George Routledge, 1855/56)

NICHOLAS BENTLEY, ed., *Russell's Despatches from the Crimea, 1854–56* (New York: Hill & Wang, Inc., 1967)

The History of *The Times* (Volume II) (New York: Kraus Reprint Co.)

J. B. ATKINS, *The Life of Sir William Howard Russell*, 2 vols. (London: John Murray, 1911)

RUPERT FURNEAUX, *The First War Correspondent* (London: Cassell & Co. Ltd, 1944)

CHRISTOPHER HIBBERT, *The Destruction of Lord Raglan* (London: Longman Ltd, 1961)

CECIL WOODHAM-SMITH, *Florence Nightingale* (New York: McGraw-Hill Book Company, 1951)

CECIL WOODHAM-SMITH, *The Reason Why* (New York: McGraw Hill Book Company, 1954; paperback ed. New York: E. P. Dutton & Co. Inc.)

PIERS COMPTON, *Colonel's Lady and Camp Follower* (London: Robert Hale Ltd, 1970)

MRS HENRY DUBERLY, *Journal Kept during the Russian War* (London: Longmans Green and Roberts, 1856)

Glossary

ABATTIS: form of defence work, made from tree-trunks with their boughs pointing outwards

ARABA: type of wagon, or cart

CANISTER: small, cast-iron shot packed into cartridges

CARABINES: kind of short rifle originally introduced for cavalry use

CARTOUCH: cartridge

CARTOUCH-BOX: waterproof container for cartridges

COATEE: short-tailed coat

COUNTERSCARP: (see SCARP)

EPAULEMENT: earth-bank used as a protection against enemy fire from the side

FASCINE: bundles of brushwood used to face walls and parapets of trenches

FAUTEUIL: arm-chair

FOUGASSE: small explosive mine, usually filled with stones

GABIONS: wicker cylinders filled with earth used for strengthening defence works

GRAPE-SHOT: small balls put several together in a bag to make scattering charge for cannon

KEPI: French military cap with horizontal peak

LINSTOCK: match-holder used in old gunnery

MAGAZINE: store for arms, ammunition, explosives and provisions

MINIÉ: rifle with grooved bore for firing lead bullets instead of a ball (as fired with a smooth-bored musket)

Glossary

PICQUET (or PICKET) : party of sentinels, or small body of troops sent out to watch for the enemy

REDOUBT : out-work or field-work without flanking defences

ROUND-SHOT : solid iron ball, sometimes weighing as much as sixty-eight pounds, capable of inflicting heavy damage and casualties

SAPPER : Private of the Royal Engineers

SCARP : sloping side of a ditch below the wall of a fortification

SHAKO : military hat, more or less cylindrical, with a peak, and upright plume or tuft

VEDETTE : mounted sentry placed in advance of an outpost

Index

Note: Numbers referring to illustrations and maps are italicized.

Index

Inkerman, 128–37, 138; hurricane devastates camp of, 140–6;
conditions during winter 1854–
55 of, 150–6, 161–3; and im-
provements in spring 1855,
164–72; expedition to Kertch
and, 173–80; 1st attack on
Redan by, 181–6; and pre-
parations for further assault,
192–4; fall of Sebastopol and,
206–16, 217, 219–20; withdrawal from Crimea of, 239–40;
late nineteenth century reforms
in, 245; Florence Nightingale's
enquiry into medical conditions
of, 246
Brontë sisters (Anne, Charlotte,
Emily), 14
Brown, Sir George (Commander
of Light Division), 31–2, 37–8,
46, 81, 83, 131, 143, 175, 179–
80, 187, 213, *32*
Bug, River, abortive sortie of
Allied ships up, 234–5
Bulgaria, 29, 41, 44, 51, 69, 100

Calamita Bay, Allied landings at,
63–9, 71, 228, *64*
Camberley Staff College, 245
Cambridge, Duke of, 86, 143, 168
Canrobert, Gen., 55, 70
Caradoc, H.M.S., 60, 130, 143
Cardigan, Brigadier-Gen. Lord
(Commander of Light Brigade),
51–3, 56, 69, 72, 106, 117, 120,
122, *52*
casualties, at Alma, 86–8, 90;
at Balaklava, 123; at Inkerman, 134–7, 142; at Tchernaya,
200, 201–2; and at Sebastopol,
186, 215, 220–2; *see also* medical
conditions
Cathcart, Gen. Sir George (Commander of 4th Division), 99, 131

Charge of the Light Brigade, *see*
Light Brigade
Chasseurs d'Afrique, 173, 195
Chenery, Thomas (*The Times*
correspondent in Constanti-
nople), 101–3
cholera epidemic, in Allied
armies, 54–8, 62, 88, 151–2;
and in fleets, 59–60; in London,
100; causes of, 100–1; *see also*
medical conditions
Clarendon, Lord (Foreign Secretary), 146
Codrington, Gen. Sir W., 213,
236–7
Commander-in-Chief of British
Army in Crimea *see* Raglan,
Lord
Commissariat, British Army, 25,
49–50, 69–70, 151, *50*; French
Army, 59
Constanta, 55, 56
Constantinople (now: Istanbul),
38, 39, 44, 101, 153, 187
Corunna, Battle of, 15
Crimea (South West), map of,
12; *see also* individual places
Crimean War, outbreak of (1854),
26; and causes of, 29–30;
peace declared (1856), 239; *see
also* individual battles, cam-
paigns

Daily News, 130
Danube, River, 44, 51
Dardanelles, 28
Dartmouth, Earl of, 188–9
Delane, John (Editor of *The
Times*), 16, 38, 46, 103–4, 128,
130, 148, 157–60, 170, 174, 175,
223, 244
Denmark, 22
Devno, 61
Dickens, Charles, 14, 22
Dickson, Lieut.-Col., 72